The COLINTON Story

Celebrating 900 years of a SCOTTISH PARISH

Lynne Gladstone-Millar

with Illustrations by Janet Munro

SAINT ANDREW PRESS
EDINBURGH

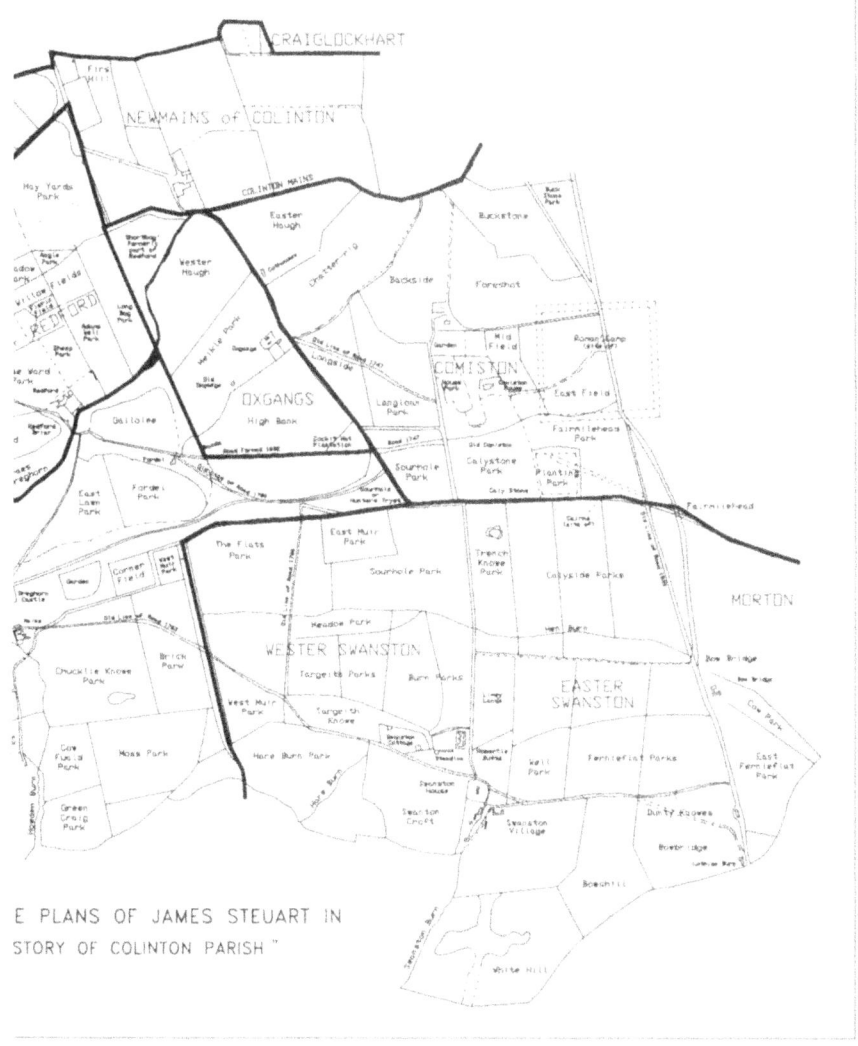

Reproduced from the 1895 Ordnance Survey Map.

First published in 1994 by
SAINT ANDREW PRESS
121 George Street, Edinburgh

on behalf of
COLINTON PARISH CHURCH
Dell Road, Edinburgh

Copyright © Colinton Parish Church 1994

ISBN: 978-0-9615319-5-9

All rights reserved. No part of this publication may be reproduced or transmitted in any form or by any means, electronic or mechanical, including photocopy, recording, or information storage and retrieval system, without permission in writing from the publisher. This book is sold, subject to the condition that it shall not, by way of trade or otherwise, be lent, re-sold, hired out or otherwise circulated without the publisher's prior consent.

British Library Cataloguing in Publication Data
A catalogue record for this book
is available from the British Library.

ISBN: 978-0-9615319-5-9

Typeset in 11.5/13 pt Garamond.
Cover design by Mark Blackadder.
Front cover photograph by Paul Turner.
Manuscript on cover by courtesy of the Trustees of the National Library of Scotland.
Printed and **bound** by Athenaeum Press Ltd, Newcastle upon Tyne.

Contents

Acknowledgments vi
Author's Note vii
Picture Credits viii

1	Credit for Heaven	1
2	Popes, Priests and Politics	15
3	Stands of Armour for the Colinton Men	27
4	Testing Times	33
5	Cromwell Comes to Colinton	42
6	The Trysting Place of all Colinton History	50
7	The Coming of the Nouveaux Riches	63
8	Smuggling at Spylaw	80
9	The National Roll-Calls	91
10	Robert Louis Stevenson Slept Here	106
11	Victorian Heyday	121
12	The Village Suburb	132
13	The Hills of Home	149

Postscript by The Revd George J Whyte 165
Appendix I: The Parish of Hailes or Colinton 167
Appendix II: The Family of Churches 169
Selected Bibliography and Sources 172
Index of Names and Places 175

Acknowledgments

THE Minister and Kirk Session of Colinton Parish Church gratefully acknowledge financial assistance from the following:

Alexander, Macaulay Associates
Bank of Scotland
CALA plc
Clydesdale Bank PLC
Mr Leslie Comrie
Mr and Mrs John Dakers
The Drummond Trust, 3 Pitt Terrace, Stirling
Dundas & Wilson, C.S.
Jenners Princes Street Edinburgh Limited
Laing the jeweller
Mactaggart & Mickel Limited
John Menzies plc
The Royal Bank of Scotland plc
Royal Mail Scotland & Northern Ireland
Ryden, Property Consultants and Chartered Surveyors
Scottish Widows Fund
G. W. Tait & Sons, S.S.C.
TSB Bank Scotland plc

and the support from the 24 Elders who participated in an interest free loan and underwriting scheme without which the publication of the book would not have been possible.

Author's Note

I SHOULD like to thank the staff of the Scottish Department and Edinburgh Room of Edinburgh Central Library for all their assistance and for the use of material held in their collections. I am also grateful to the staffs of the Historical Search Room of the Scottish Record Office, the National Library of Scotland, the Royal Commission on the Ancient and Historical Monuments of Scotland and Colinton Public Library for their patience and help. In addition, my thanks go to the Colinton Local History Society and to Colinton Parish Church for the use of their archive material.

Local historians Frances Bennetts, Frank Bennetts and Mary Harris have given generously of their time and expertise in this project, as have John Arnott and David Stranock with the photography, and I have appreciated this so much. I also wish to thank Catherine Foggo for compiling the Colinton Family of Churches (Appendix II), Stewart Cruden for his expert advice on masons' marks, Karine Macaulay for Parish Magazine research, and Surveys & Development Services of 3 Hope Street, Bo'ness, for the digital mapping on the maps of the Colinton Estates and the Development of Colinton.

Every effort has been made to find the owners of copyright of material in this book, but should any reader have knowledge of copyright not found, then at second reprint this will be included.

Lynne Gladstone-Millar

Picture Credits

THE *photographs and illustrations in the chapters listed below are reproduced by courtesy of the following:*

CHAPTER 1: *The Great Rock* on page 9, Edinburgh City Libraries; *Medieval Gravestones* on page 10, The Society of Antiquaries of Scotland.

CHAPTER 2: *Pontifical Offices* on page 17 (both), Bibliothèque Nationale, Paris.

CHAPTER 3: *Colinton Castle* on page 31, Edinburgh City Libraries.

CHAPTER 5: *Kirk Session Minutes of Colinton Parish Ref. CH2/123* on page 47, The Principal Clerk of The General Assembly of The Church of Scotland with the approval of The Keeper of the Records of Scotland.

CHAPTER 6: Map extract from *'The Shyres Lothian and Linlitquo'* by *T. Pont, Mercator Atlas 1630* on page 53, Bartholomew, Edinburgh; *Redford House* on page 59, Edinburgh City Libraries.

CHAPTER 7: *Graysmill Farm and Fernielaw sketch* on page 69, Edinburgh City Libraries; *Roy's Military Survey of Scotland, 1747* on page 76, The British Library; *Plan of the Farm in the Parish of Collington belonging to Jas. Gillespie,* Ref. RHP47 on page 77, The Keeper of Records of Scotland with the agreement of The Controller of Her Majesty's Stationery Office.

CHAPTER 8: *Spylaw House* on page 80, Edinburgh City Libraries; *Bank of Scotland Note* on page 82, The Bank of Scotland; *Redhall Mill* on page 83, Edinburgh City Libraries; *The Revd Robert Walker, Skating on Duddingston Loch, by Sir Henry Raeburn* on page 88 (top), courtesy of The National Gallery of Scotland; *Kirk Session Minutes of Colinton Parish Ref. CH2/123* on page

88 (bottom), The Principal Clerk of The General Assembly of The Church of Scotland with the approval of The Keeper of the Records of Scotland.

CHAPTER 9: *Dreghorn Castle* on page 94, Edinburgh City Libraries; *Colinton Farm* on page 95, the CA Magazine; *Bonaly Tower by D. O. Hill* on page 97, The Scottish National Portrait Gallery (Photographic Archive).

CHAPTER 10: *R.L.S. Signature* and *Baby Book* on pages 106 (bottom) and 108 (top), Edinburgh City Libraries; *Henry Mackenzie, by Colvin Smith* on page 118, courtesy of The Scottish National Portrait Gallery.

CHAPTER 11: *Heritors' Minutes, Ref. HR728* on page 121 (text), The Principal Clerk of The General Assembly of The Church of Scotland with the approval of The Keeper of the Records of Scotland; *Colinton Cottage* on page 125 (top), The Royal Commission on the Ancient and Historical Monuments of Scotland; *Drummond Scrolls* on page 125 (bottom), Edinburgh City Libraries; *The Cottage Homes* on page 131, The Aged Christian Friend Society of Scotland.

CHAPTER 12: *Pillar Detail* on page 135, David Stranock; *Tram Terminus* on page 142, Edinburgh City Libraries;

CHAPTER 13: *The Revd Marion Dodd* on page 151, R. Clapperton, Selkirk; *The Queen in Colinton* on page 156, courtesy of The Scotsman Publications Ltd; *Ceremonial March-in* on page 158, Mark Owens, Photographic Officer for the Army, Scotland; *Bonaly Primary School* on page 162, David Stranock.

Acknowledgments for Colour Section

Aerial Photographs of Colinton, Johnstone Syer Photography, Dunfermline.

The Development of Colinton Map is reproduced by courtesy of Ordnance Survey and the digital mapping is by Surveys & Development Services of Bo'ness.

Armorial Bearings of Colinton Parish Church, photograph by Paul Turner.

David I's confirmation of the gift of his brother Ethelred, The Trustees of The National Library of Scotland.

St Cuthbert's Tomb, The Dean and Chapter of Durham Cathedral.
Colinton Village, Robert Ferguson.
The Very Revd W. B. Johnston, Studio Jay Photography.
The Revd George J. Whyte, Simon Jones.

CHAPTER 1

Credit for Heaven

THE Colinton story starts nine hundred years ago. Today it is a commuter suburb of Edinburgh, sprawling from Juniper Green in the west, to Kingsknowe in the north and Oxgangs in the east. In the south, its boundary line marches over the rolling hills of the Pentlands, taking in its stride reservoirs, sheep pastures and wooded slopes. Colinton is an area of Georgian cottages, Victorian villas, army barracks, modern housing estates, ancient manors and open countryside.

Through all the tides of progress and set-back which it has seen across the centuries – in farming, in industry along the Water of Leith, in transport, and in its enormous growth over the last couple of generations – the area has had one strand of continuity: the parish church. It has seen the Disruption of the Church, Covenanting violence, and reforming upheaval, but all the way back to Medieval times the church has given its parish a sense of place. Even today, within a great city, Colinton still has the identity of a village.

Nine hundred years ago the area was a bleak moorland. Little groups of simple turf dwellings, thatched with the reeds from the bog at Redhall or the Reed-ford at Bonaly Burn, clustered round the sheltered valleys of the Water of Leith or clung to the slopes of the Pentlands where the land was drier.

There had been people in these parts for a long time – a Celtic tribe, whom the Romans had called the Votadini, had settlements at Dumbryden, between the Water of Leith and the Murray Burn, and there was an Iron Age fort on Wester Craiglockhart Hill. It had never, however, been easy to survive here, and in 1095 the people eked out a mean livelihood by herding a few cattle, hunting game, cutting peats for fuel and growing small patches of bere barley and oats. They also made cheese out of ewes' milk, garnered honey and brewed ale, and the womenfolk and girls spun and wove the coarse plaids which everyone wore.

There was nothing idyllic about this rural life. The inhabitants of Colinton nine centuries ago not only lived in constant fear of disease and hunger, but of other hazards as well. Wolves might attack their animals if they were not properly guarded by the boys; William Rufus – the Norman-English king – might come storming north, rampaging round the Pentland foothills, showing little mercy to those who stood in his way; and then opportunist marauding bands in search of captives to sell as slaves might at any time ambush the cot-houses. (Slaves were not only excellent bargaining counters, but were useful for dowry gifts or giving as presents to soul-hungry monasteries.)

The well-being of the soul was a continual preoccupation of the people, although making extravagant gestures to ensure a gilt-edged salvation could only be a privilege of the rich. If the monks could be given a serf to help with the manual tasks around the monastery, that would be remembered at Judgment Day, but if they could be given the land for a whole church – well, that would amount to a great deal of credit for heaven.

For the Colinton people, however, there was not much security for the after-life. They had no church to pray in and the most they could ever hope for was that a wandering monk would give them a blessing or two, or say a mass for their souls when they died. It was believed that there had at one time been an ancient chapel at Hailes, which early missionary Christians had founded; but that had gone long ago, the monks being victims, like so many other local inhabitants, of pillaging pirates and foraging vandals.

A surprise benefaction, however, was to change all this. Into this meagre community one day clattered a royal procession on horseback. Prince Ethelred, a younger son of King Malcolm Canmore and Queen Margaret, had come not only to gather his dues from the Lands of Hailes, given to him some years earlier by his father, but to choose a site for a church which he proposed to found and give to the monks of the Church of the Holy Trinity at Dunfermline. To present the new church at Hailes to Dunfermline was a natural decision – Ethelred's mother had founded a religious community there and he had grown up in the palace next door to it. Ethelred was also the Comes (the Earl) of Fife.

There were particularly pressing reasons for this young Scottish prince, who was only in his early twenties at the time, to think in terms of founding a church. In 1093 Ethelred's father had been killed and his eldest brother mortally wounded in an ambush in Northumberland, and his mother, her body weakened by obsessive religious observances and fastings, had died in Edinburgh Castle a few days later.

In the ensuing power struggle for the throne, Ethelred had had the unnerving experience of smuggling his mother's body out of the Castle in order to get it over to Dunfermline for a decent burial by the monks. Andrew de Wyntoun, writing in his *Orygynale Cronykil of Scotland* in the fourteenth century, described graphically Ethelred's furtive journey out of the Castle in the mist; and in the recent excavations at the Castle, when an entrance tunnel was made, the paved causeway over which he hurried his precious burden was uncovered.

ETHELRED'S SEARCH FOR A SITE
FOR A CHURCH ENDED AT HAILES

It was always a very unsafe business being a son of a king – of the last twelve kings of Alba, only one had not died a violent death, and sons of kings were killed by usurpers as a matter of course to eliminate accession problems. Ethelred's father, Malcolm Canmore, had slaughtered and slain his way to the throne – one of his victims being Macbeth – and upon Canmore's death there was no shortage of claimants who wanted to see the Canmore heirs out of the way. In addition, Ethelred's educated, saintly mother, Queen Margaret, made no secret of the fact that she would rather have been a nun than a wife. She had taught her children how important it was to make provision for having masses said for their souls, and how essential it was to have somewhere sacred for the placing of their dead bodies and those of their families, from which they could be resurrected with grace.

The fear of sudden death, therefore, would drive Prince Ethelred, even at his young age, to make appropriate preparations. In addition, he may have felt he should do the right thing by his late father, mother and brother, and found a church to commemorate them.

Matters outside Scotland may also have had a profound effect upon Ethelred. In 1095 religious turmoil swept across Europe. Pope Urban II, by preaching the First Crusade at Clermont, sparked off a migration eastwards in the next two years of nearly a hundred thousand people who, for reasons of their own, had 'taken the Cross'. Adventuring knights from Scotland went. From nearby Rosslyn, Henry de Saint-Clair rushed off to join Godfroi de Bouillon when his army of Crusaders set out from Verdun. Ethelred's uncle, Edgar Atheling, heard about the Crusade at his sister's court in Dunfermline and, gathering a band around him, set forth for the Holy Land. Ethelred himself did not go. Was the church at Hailes given to God instead of service on Crusade?

At home, Ethelred already had a connection with the church, for ever since he had been merely a boy he had been the lay abbot of Dunkeld. He had inherited this abbacy through the line of Crinan, his great-grandfather, who, embroiled to the hilt in the succession struggles at the time of King Macbeth, had had no qualms about merging his role as abbot with that of soldier, and had in fact died in battle.

In the main, however, the abbacy was a source of unearned income in teinds – a tenth portion of all produce and stock traditionally exacted by the Church. Lay abbots could marry, as Crinan had done, and not much was expected of them by way of religious duties. Whether Ethelred regarded his abbacy as a pleasant sinecure, or whether he had inherited his mother's daunting piety, is impossible to say, but here he now was in Colinton, motivated by countless obligations, determined to found the church of St Cuthbert which was destined to be the nucleus of the village for centuries to come.

His first instructions about the church to his personal retinue would be in Gaelic, for he grew up in Fife in a Gaelic-speaking court. However, the folk in Colinton would not understand him, as they spoke in Cumbric, a language rooted in Old Welsh which had seeped north to them and was to become an early Lowland Scots language in its own right. Ethelred would also describe his gift of land as being in Hailes, for the area was not known as Colinton until the fourteenth century.

Ethelred's charter containing the details of his gift to the church at Dunfermline no longer exists, but in the *Registrum de Dunfermlyne* there is, in meticulous brown lettering, the confirmation by his brother, David I, of various family gifts, including the words '*Dona Ethelredi fris mei, Hales*' – Hales, the gifts of my brother Ethelred. This charter is dated *circa* 1128.

Down through the mists of time the site of Hailes House has been mantled with the folklore that it was there that the first Church of Hailes stood. Certainly it would be a convenient site for a church in that there were reeds at the Redhall bog for thatching, stone nearby for quarrying and a well for the priest when he moved into his small lean-to hut. Below Hailes House in the Dell there is a sizeable hollow quarried out among the outcrops of stone and it is quite conceivable that it was from here that the workmen who built the new church took their stone.

In addition, on the cobbled driveway and in the rockeries of the house that was formerly the stableyard of Hailes House, there are stones with Medieval masons' marks incised on them, dated from a time much earlier than the building of Hailes House which was around 1765. Builders at that time were always economical with materials, and they re-used stones for many purposes. These particular stones point to a building of some importance being in the vicinity from at least Medieval times.

The existence of what was known as the Hailes Altar Stone also gave credence in Victorian times to the idea that the first

church was on the site of Hailes House. Built into the garden wall of Hailes House, the stone was identified by experts in 1918 as being a sculpture of the Three Mother Goddesses – the *Matres* – worshipped in the earliest centuries AD.

The stone was set up in Scotland by Roman troops in the second century, and is held to be one of the finest examples of its kind in Europe. Perhaps it was originally at the Roman fort at Cramond and was brought to Hailes to embellish a country mansion, a custom of the seventeenth century *nouveaux riches*; or perhaps it had always been at Hailes, the altar of a smaller contingent of Roman soldiers far from home. There is some evidence that the Romans were at Colinton. Roman artefacts have been found on the Pentlands and near Colinton, and they had a camp at Comiston. In addition, a paved way at Boag's Mill, still visible at the end of last century, was thought to date from Roman times.

The Hailes Altar Stone itself, however, depicting three figures holding baskets of fruit and ears of corn, and draped in robes and shawls which were clearly not Scottish dress, was mistaken for a representation of the Holy Trinity. Even a minister of Colinton, at the end of the nineteenth century, wrote of the stone: 'Above a doorway in a wall in the garden of Hailes House, to the west of that house, there is a rude stone, with three seated figures on it, evidently representing the Holy Trinity.'

It is not surprising that the stone at Hailes was associated with the first church building, because it was to the Church of the Holy Trinity at Dunfermline that Ethelred had given it. The stone is now in the safe-keeping of the monks of the abbey at Fort Augustus, to whom it was given in the 1930s by the then owner of Hailes House, when it became a Youth Hostel. The monks, fully aware of its pagan origin, do not however refer to it as the Hailes Altar Stone, but firmly call it the Roman Three Goddesses Stone and, appreciating its historical importance, they have carefully built it into an inside eighteenth century wall at the abbey.

At the beginning of the nineteenth century the legend that the church was sited in the vicinity of Hailes House was put into print. George Chalmers in his *Caledonia* wrote in 1810: 'The Mansion of Hailes, where the ancient church stood ....' But he gave no source for his claim. The Revd Lewis Balfour repeated the assertion in 1838 in *The Statistical Account of Edinburghshire*, but he was more cautious: 'Some have stated, on what grounds I know not, that the church once stood where the mansion house of Hailes at present stands.' The Revd William Lockhart, writing in *The Proceedings of the Society of Antiquaries* in 1883, was content to accept the statement of Chalmers, as was John Geddie in his book on the Water of Leith. David Shankie in *The Parish of Colinton*, published in 1902, wrote: 'Hailes House, supposed, and upon which most of those interested in the history of the parish are agreed, to be the site of the parish church in Medieval times ...', and this view was repeated by J A Scott in *Portrait of a Parish*. The date for the removal of the church from Hailes to its present site in the Dell is generally given as 1636, or around 1650.

Further research, however, makes a strong case for the church to have been in the Dell probably from its foundation, or at least very much earlier than the seventeenth century. The first recorded priest of Hailes is Magister Ricardus de Moravia. Master Richard may have been only a vicar, a vice-priest with the Abbot of Dunfermline as his superior, but he was not afraid to fight for the dues of his church. This may have been because, as a vicar, he had no right to the teinds of his parish, or to a fixed income out of the benefice; for his bread and butter he had to depend on the benevolence of the monks in Dunfermline who may have set aside for him a proportion of the Colinton folks' eggs, fowls, hay and lint, but who were not obliged to do so.

In 1226, therefore, Master Richard came into dispute with Thomas of Lastalric – now Restalrig – concerning ownership of the mill and the mill pond behind the church. The final outcome and agreement is meticulously recorded by a monk in the *Registrum de Dunfermlyne*, scribing in the customary shorthand cartulary Latin, but with a couple of very human lapses into the Medieval French in which he was thinking. Was the writer a French monk, perhaps, homesick for the Paris where he was trained?

The agreement is so relevant to the siting of the early church that it is worth translating part of it:

> *In the Year of Our Lord 1226, on the day of St. Faith the Virgin, this final agreement was made between Thomas of Lastalric on the one side and Master Richard, Parson of Hailes, in the name of the church of Hailes on the other side, with the consent and assent of Lord William Abbot and the convent of Dunfermline, that is that the said Thomas and his heirs shall have the mill pond of Hailes as that pond was on the aforesaid day so that they shall not extend their pond towards the land of the church more than it was on that day.*
>
> *The said Thomas and his heirs shall also have the mill with Midelhope and Milncroft as far as the great rock (usque ad grossam petram) as the aforesaid Thomas had on that day. They and their men shall also have free access and exit to the mill by the highway. The parson, however, shall have in the name of the church from the aforesaid great rock the whole remainder of the land as far as the ditch* [or dyke] *which was made in ancient times as a boundary with the half Seijill'un* [a French word for a rig of land] *in the direction of the 'faleijs'* [another French word meaning cliff or steep gorge] *as the Lord Hugh, Bishop of Dunkeld and the Lord William, Abbot of Dunfermline, provided on that day and the aforesaid church shall also have that small parcel of land which lies between the garden of the church and the highway, which runs towards the mill. Saving also to the church the lands and possessions which it owned on that day peacefully ....*

The threat of fearsome penalties follows, including excommunication, if either side should break the agreement.

An examination of the terrain behind the present church reveals that the topographical details so precisely given in the 1226 document match up well with what exists there today, and the mill referred to was in all probability the Hole Mill, the remains of which can still be seen behind the manse. A 'great rock' (*grossa petra*) juts out of the Water of Leith and rears up to the skyline of the Dell. The boundary ditch or dyke may have followed the line round the edge of the old cemetery, and it is significant that this demarcation is described as 'in ancient times', implying that it existed long before Master Richard's day in 1226. In addition there is space in the hollow of the valley there for a parcel of land between a church garden and a highway that would run down to the mill. The terrain of Hailes House, on the other hand, cannot be reconciled so readily with these geographical features.

There is also the question of the bridge at the foot of Spylaw Street. In early times, of course, there was no bridge, but a ford. By 1575, however, the record of the will of Sir Andro Binning described him as 'vicar of the Kirk at the Brig of Haillis'. It is not known exactly when Sir Andro became vicar of Haillis, but his testament shows that he was living at Haillis when he died.

In 1585 the Borthwick family were chronicled as having built a mansion house at 'Kirklands of Haillies' on the site of the present

'Usque ad Grossam Petram' – as far as the Great Rock – states Master Richard's 1226 Land Agreement. The Great Rock is still seen across the Water of Leith, behind Colinton Manse.

new cemetery, and in 1594 the Register of the Great Seal referred to the church lands of Hailes as '*et omnes incorporavit in tenandriam de Haillisbrig*' – the lands of Haillisbrig. The first bridge across the river at Colinton would surely have been at the site of the ford – at present-day Hailes the gorge is too steep to be suitable.

Thomas's mill came into prominence again very significantly in 1630, when the Great Seal referred to *'Terras de Eister Haillis (exceptis molendino et terris molendinariis ad tergum ecclesiae de Haillis)'* – the lands of Easter Hailes except the mill and the lands of the mill *at the back of the Church of Hailes*. A mill has to be beside a river, and at Hailes House the river does not run nearby, but is some distance away, down a very steep bank. At the Dell site, on the other hand, the church and manse lie in the elbow of the river – ideal territory for mills.

Another argument for the Dell site is that for some time a fourteenth or fifteenth century recumbent grave slab belonging to a person of some standing, perhaps a Knight Templar, stood propped against an outside wall of the church. The Revd Lewis Balfour, in his contribution on Colinton to *The Statistical Account of Edinburghshire*, wrote in 1838: 'Part of the cover of a stone coffin was lately taken out of the rubbish in the floor of the church. It bears on it the rude outlines of a sword and mace, the latter consisting of a simple handle, and ending in four circles, meeting in a common centre.'

One of two grave slabs photographed outside the church in 1905 answers this description. An examination of the photograph by modern experts reveals that they believe it would not have

been in such good condition if it had been lying outside for centuries. In 1914 both stones were moved inside the church on the advice of an expert from the Royal Commission on the Ancient and Historical Monuments of Scotland, but some time after that they mysteriously disappeared.

And furthermore, there still

exists the tablet of Agnes Heriot, now inside the church, which is dated 1593. These stones indicate that there was a burial place in the Dell well before the middle of the seventeenth century, probably within the vaults of a building. In addition, graveyards were customarily put beside the church.

There is a long-standing belief that a new church was built in the Dell in about 1630, replacing an old one, but there is no clear evidence of this. It may have been built by Sir James Foulis of Colinton; by that time the local landowners had taken on the role of providing churches for the community. Sir James's fine sundial, dated 1630, can still be read on the present church building. As for the manse, a stone incised with the date 1636 set into its wall was from an earlier building, for the existing manse was built in 1784.

Finally, the vault beneath the present church has been dated as from the 1600s, with a door leading originally up to an aisle inside a building above. The ghosting of shelves for the coffins can still be seen inside the vault. The masons of the subsequent church buildings which were put up on the same site have simply built on top of it.

It is very likely that Ethelred's church was built of stone. As far back as *circa* AD 400 Ninian had built his stone Candida Casa at Whithorn, and in 710 Nechtan, King of the Picts in Angus, had sent to Ceolfrith, the Abbot of Jarrow, asking for monks to come north and tell his men how to build a church of stone. The stone round tower in Brechin had stood since 1020, and in Orkney the Celtic missionaries had built with stone. Ethelred's parents had been married in 1070 in Malcolm's little plastered stone church in Dunfermline, a small rectangular cell of Celtic design embellished with a western tower – the church which Margaret enlarged and dedicated to the Holy Trinity. St Margaret's Chapel at Edinburgh Castle was a sturdy stone building erected by Ethelred's brother only about a couple of decades after the Church of Hailes. It is possible, of course, that the first Church of Hailes was a small wooden building with a thatched roof, but this was a royal foundation which the young prince would want to last. Therefore he would surely insist upon the local stone.

A definite link with the little Church of Hailes from its earliest times to the present day is its name: St Cuthbert's. For Ethelred to dedicate his church to St Cuthbert was a bold political statement – his was no Columban foundation. In order to understand the significance of this, it is necessary to look for a moment into the history of the early Scottish Church. Christianity had reached South West Scotland by the fifth century, much of the early conversion work being associated with Ninian. After his death, other missionaries took over, and two centuries later Columba spread the word further from his base in Iona. This infant Celtic Church was by its very nature fragmented – Columba emphasised the importance of personal devotion rather than of institutionalised worship – and this was to be its undoing. Over the centuries the highly structured Church of Rome was to work actively to overwhelm the Celtic Church and its quaint ways, and at the Synod of Whitby in 664, when the two factions confronted each other, the Roman party prevailed. One of the Celtic-trained priests who changed to the Roman customs after the decree of Whitby was Cuthbert.

The Romanising of the Church not only suited the Pope and his ambitious archbishops, but it also appealed to some of the Scottish kings, who could see that there was an advantage to be gained from alliance with the powerful Church of Rome. King Macbeth in his time even went on a much publicised pilgrimage to Rome, although he never quite revealed if this also involved a private conversion to Christianity. Ingibjorg, Malcolm Canmore's first queen, did not live long, but his second queen, Margaret, turned firmly to Rome, and she was to prove as purposeful a lady in her ambitions as had her predecessor a decade before, Queen Gruoch – Lady Macbeth.

Brought up in Hungary and England, Margaret could not reconcile herself to the Celtic form of worship which she found in Scotland. She was, in fact, so convinced of the correctness of Romish ways that when she married Canmore she saw her vocation as a personal crusade to have the Roman Church fully established in the kingdom.

Although she never persecuted the few Columban establishments which were left, she succeeded entirely in having her way. Malcolm, infatuated by his beautiful flaxen-haired queen, happily interpreted for her at the court in Dunfermline when she discussed these religious matters with the Gaelic-speaking priests whom she found there, and supported her when she requested help from the Archbishop of Canterbury for her church foundation. Ethelred, when he carried on his mother's tradition of founding a church, dedicated it to the Scottish saint who had most met with her approval – St Cuthbert.

Cuthbert, although he ended his career as the Bishop of Lindisfarne, had humble beginnings as a shepherd boy on the Lammermuir Hills. Upon a sudden religious experience, he forsook the hills for the monastery of Old Melrose, where he received his training. However, he never forgot his love of solitude and he spent much of his adult life as a hermit on a neck of land near Holy Island, and later on Inner Farne. He was fetched out of his contemplative life by his superiors to be in charge firstly of the see of Hexham, and latterly of Lindisfarne, but it is said that he packed into this life innumerable journeyings over the Border hills dispensing a miracle here, a soul-saving there. Perhaps he was homesick for Scotland.

When St Cuthbert died in 687, he was not brought home to the Lammermuir Hills. It is thought that at first he was buried at Lindisfarne, but for safety reasons his body was later moved to Chester-le-Street when the Danes were pillaging the area. He was then shunted around north-east England, one step ahead of the invaders, until he was finally deposited in a fine shrine at Durham Cathedral.

There is an intriguing legend, however, that at the Reformation, when Henry VIII was on the rampage, Durham Cathedral was again considered unsafe for Cuthbert, and he was moved once more. The story is that only the Benedictines know where St Cuthbert's final resting place is, and only three monks at a time learn the exact spot.

Naturally over the centuries, the clergy at Durham Cathedral have never been keen to give up their saint to such folklore, and in 1827, and again in 1899, the coffin behind the high altar, always reputed to be Cuthbert's, was exhumed. Fragments of vestments and a cross, together with medical reports, convinced the experts at that time that it was indeed Cuthbert who lay safely in honour at Durham. Up to today the clergy have found no Benedictines who refute this.

As for Prince Ethelred himself – where was he buried? Most sources agree that he died young. George Grub in his *Ecclesiastical History of Scotland*, published in 1861, asserts that he was probably dead by 1097, and by 1107 he is referred to in a deed recorded in the Register of the Prior of St Andrews as a 'man of venerated memory'. Andrew de Wyntoun, writing in the fourteenth century, states that Ethelred was buried in Dunfermline, but there have been excavations this century of five graves within the foundations of Margaret's church in Dunfermline and it is assumed that these graves are the final resting places of Margaret, Malcolm (who was brought there from Northumberland where he was killed), and their sons Edward, Edgar and Alexander. Of the other sons, Edmund, who repented from a black-sheep period by becoming a monk, died in the south of England, and David I, who built a new church in Dunfermline, was buried before its high altar.

Sir James Balfour, writing in his *Annales of Scotland* in 1630, claimed that Ethelred was interred in the old church in St Andrews 'because he was a great benefactor to that monastery'. Another resting place for Ethelred, of course, could have been his own Abbey of Dunkeld – there are still some very ancient stones there which are believed to have marked important, if not royal, graves. On the other hand, however, Ethelred might have wished to be buried in the church of his own endowment, that of St Cuthbert at Hailes. With the Water of Leith tumbling by and the birds singing in the Dell, here, perhaps, lies Ethelred.

CHAPTER 2

Popes, Priests and Politics

HOW did the establishment of Ethelred's church affect the small settlements scattered around on the lands of Hailes? How did its influence rub off on the lives of its peoples?

In the first place, it meant that this tiny community in an outpost of Europe was put on the map in Rome. The original priests to minister to Colinton were sent from the monastery next door to the palace in Dunfermline. They came over on Ethelred's mother's ferry, the Queen's Ferry, and crossed the empty lands of Dalmeny and Kirkliston, fording the Almond and the Gogar Burn and turning towards the valley of the Water of Leith.

Into the little church they put patens of pewter and cups of silver, which amazed the local people who were accustomed to eating off wooden platters and drinking from crude beakers of horn or wood. Even the abundance of candles astonished them.

As yet there was no structured parish system, and while a monk or priest may have been assigned permanently to the church at Hailes, and lived there in a lean-to hut or a simple dwelling with a turfed roof, the whole organisation was worked from the monastery at Dunfermline whose abbot was answerable finally to Rome. It was not until the influence of the Anglo-Normans filtered north that Scotland came to be divided into a parish system, the churches and priests being maintained by the exaction of tithes and the offerings of pious parishioners. Bishops ruled these dioceses from their cathedral churches, and monastic orders such as the Benedictines, who occupied the Dunfermline Abbey foundation of David I, provided training and manpower for the field. The Dunfermline monks had superiority over the church at Hailes and authority to collect its tithes until the early thirteenth century, when their abbot was unwise enough to fall out with his bishop over a question of the quality of the wine at dinner, and the patronage of Hailes was summarily given to the canons of Holyrood Abbey.

While King Malcolm and Queen Margaret had tolerated the remnants of the Celtic Church, their son David, the 'Sair Sanct for the Croun', had less patience, and he lost no time in putting Norman bishops and abbots, who used the Romish traditions, into as many churches and monasteries as possible. The folk of Colinton, therefore, got their absolutions and their blessings in the Latin of the Pope. Even their priest had a Latin name – the 'vicarius'. He was called this because he was a vice-priest acting on behalf of the Abbot of Dunfermline. This vicar, like all the others in the country, was appointed by the authority of the Pope, and each nomination was punctiliously recorded in papal bulls, many of which survive to this day. In the Vatican there was a bureaucracy whose tentacles reached all over Europe.

Distance seemed to be no barrier. Horsemen with dispatch bags travelled regularly between Scotland and the ecclesiastical clearing house in Paris, from where documents were sent on for the papal seal at Rome, Florence or Avignon, wherever the Pope of the day happened to be.

BISHOP DAVID DE BERNHAM

... CONSECRATING 140 CHURCHES IN THE NEXT NINE YEARS.

Initially the Scottish Church did not have archbishops of her own, and the power-hungry Archbishop of York liked to consider that the Scots were under his control. While this suited Queen Margaret, who had looked to England for material help in her church work, it did not suit the local churchmen and the warring barons of later years. In 1192, after much politicking by the Scottish bishops, the Scottish Church shook itself free of

English dominance and became a 'special daughter' of the papacy. In issuing this very significant bull, Pope Celestine III dismissed for all time any claims from York or Canterbury to superiority over the Scottish Church.

Thus the Scottish Church had gained her identity, but because she still had no archbishops, her ten bishops were subject directly to the Pope. To keep the system running smoothly, papal legates were sent to see that everything was in order, and in 1239, at the Legatine Council in Edinburgh, the Pope's representative, Cardinal Otho, expressed his great concern at the fact that so many of the Scottish churches had never been consecrated. This galvanised Bishop David de Bernham of St Andrews into action, and, beginning at Lasswade, he galloped up and down the country consecrating 140 churches in the next nine years. The Church of Hailes was consecrated towards the end of this hectic round, on 27th September 1248 – the date is jotted down by David de Bernham in the margin of his Pontifical, now in the archives in Paris. Previous to this day, however, the bishop had made a private visit to Hailes, perhaps with not quite so much pomp. Before a consecration, he had to satisfy himself that the church's roof did not leak, that there were the necessary communion plate, chalice and font, enough candles, and that the priest had the proper books and vestments. The Church of Hailes must have reached the required standard for consecration. This is the prayer David de Bernham used:

A DOODLE ON DAVID DE BERNHAM'S PONTIFICAL – A SELF-PORTRAIT?

To thee, Holy Trinity, one God, we commend the care of this temple which we have consecrated to thee, our only Lord God, that thou mayest standest here our protector, and receive the bows and prayers

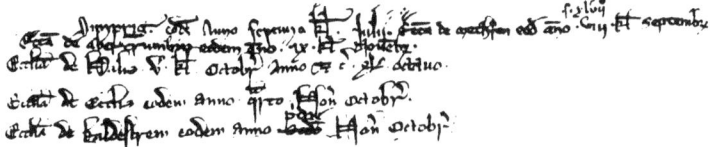

CONSECRATION DATE, WRITTEN IN THE MARGIN OF THE PONTIFICAL – HALE, 27TH SEPTEMBER 1248.

THE ARRIVAL OF THE BISHOP AND HIS RETINUE

of the worshippers, and abide the most watchful guardian and immoveable defender of this thy holy house, opposing the shield of thy divine protection against the enemy of mankind, lest the author of evil infect the holy prayers and vows made here.

But under thy defence, O Holy Trinity, to whose care we commend this house, all that pray in this place, protected by the shield of thy defence from all hurt of body and soul, shall be heard.

Deign also to receive the prayers of the Christian people on the highest throne of thy majesty; who, one in a perfect Trinity, livest and art glorified, God for ever and ever.

On the day of the ceremony, the arrival of the bishop and his retinue in their splendid consecration robes must have been awe-inspiring for the people crowding round the little Church of Hailes. The consecration rite was grand. In Latin, of course, the Pontifical Offices were lengthy, and there were responses set to music. Holy water was sprinkled on the stones where the consecration crosses were to be carved. Candles were lit and incense swung. Perhaps the Missa de Sancto Cuthbert was sung, a mass for the saint to whom the church was dedicated. The community would not have seen anything like it before, and it would have been long talked about in the dwellings around the Dell.

Two years later the people had another memorable service in the church at Hailes. In 1250 the founder's mother, Queen

Margaret, was canonised and services of thanksgiving were held throughout the country to celebrate the elevation of this remarkable Scottish queen to sainthood.

Although the way of life was still meagre for the villagers, the church at Hailes had become a rich foundation. The taxation table of the churches in the Archdeanery of Lothian and Deanery of Linlithgow enumerates that whereas Hailes was rated at 60 merks, St Giles in Edinburgh was only 26 merks, Kinleith (Currie) 50 and Pentland 12. The wealthiest church in the neighbourhood was the one whose parish boundaries marched with those of Hailes, St Cuthbert's-by-the-Castle – rated at 160 merks.

Inextricably bound up with the strength of the Church was the power of the Norman barons who began settling in Scotland from the time of David I. They contributed not only many French words to the Scots language, but much wealth to the Church. They, like their royal masters, appreciated the wisdom of making good provision for their souls. Often, if there were no church in the vicinity, they built one on their own land, or, if there was a church, they might give it a further endowment. Ethelred's church, for instance, benefited in 1226 when Pope Honorius III confirmed to the monks at Holyrood '*terram in Hales juxta fluvium Goger quam Ricardus filius Audoenj ecclesiae vestrae pia liberalitate donavit*' – the land in Hailes next to the Gogar stream which had been given out of goodness and generosity to the church by Audoenus' son, Richard.

While the local church was being enriched, however, the local people were not. The struggle to keep body and soul together continued to be their total preoccupation. On the day of the fair, they sold hides, cheeses and perhaps a hen or two, but most of the food they could grow or garner they needed for the family. Their diet was still simple and repetitive: cheese made from ewe-milk, meat if the hunting had been good, dried fish, bannocks, barley-bread, honey, gruel, home-brewed ale and brose. Blades for their knives and platters for their meals, they bought from the packmen who came travelling through the Dell.

Bartering was haphazard, so their sovereign, David I, had decreed that a uniform standard of weights and measures should be used. An inch was henceforth to be precisely the length of three grains of bere set end to end (clean and without 'tailyis') or the width of a man's thumb at the root of the nail, averaged over the thumbs of three men. Coins, which were replacing the bartering system, were also to be exact. When the people were handling coins, they were to be sure that one shilling weighed 32 grains of 'good and round wheat'.

There was little time for leisure for old or young. Food-growing had become more of a co-operative business. The men worked together, but not very economically, it seems. Usually their small strips of land – the run-rigs – were scattered all over the farming area. A team of eight or ten oxen pulled each clumsy wooden plough, and the measure of land they worked on was called an 'oxgang', an eighth of a ploughgate, the area reckoned to be what a ploughteam could work in one year. In practice, an oxgang in south-east Scotland was generally measured as 13 acres.

Wood-gathering for building and fuel was also an essential task for the cottar-folk, and this was time-consuming because  timber was scarce. When the presence of wolves had been such a daily threat to their flocks, the people made a practice of cutting down the trees which harboured the animals. Other day-to-day foraging for timber with little, if any, replanting, had over the centuries made the land around Colinton virtually denuded of trees.

Shepherding and the guarding of animals was a job given to the boys in the families, and they not only had to look after their own flocks, but, by royal decree, help the local baron to guard his herds as well. While the boys were in the fields, the girls had to help their mothers with the spinning and dyeing of wool and the washing of clothes on the flat stones at the side of the Water of Leith.

King David I was a keen advocate of the feudal system. The consequence of feudalism where it was established was that every man had to become the vassal of a lord, which meant having to farm for him and fight for him. The vassals' lot was better, but only marginally, than that of the slaves attached to many baronial households, who could be sold like cattle. These slaves were often

Northumbrian prisoners-of-war captured in raids over the Border, and the children of these slaves were born into serfdom. Indeed it was not until the Wars of Independence (1296–1357) that serfdom died out here, but Scotland led the way in Europe in this respect.

It was natural that barons seeking land should look at the area of Colinton. It was near the seat of government, near the Queen's Ferry on the Forth, and it was within reach of the trading port of Leith. It was not long, therefore, before the men of Colinton had lords forcing them to be vassals.

THE GIRLS WERE OCCUPIED WITH SPINNING AND WEAVING.

Around the year 1190 the monks at Dunfermline, always with an eye to good husbandry, decided to feu out the lands of Hailes to Sir Archibald Douglas. The next landlords of these feus were the Logans of Rastalrig – later to be known as Restalrig.

Names familiar in today's parish began to appear early in the thirteenth century. Redhall was the first Barony in Colinton and its lands covered a wide area south-east of the Water of Leith across to Craiglockhart. Documents from the reign of Alexander III (1249–1286) record that a William Le Grant, who came north from Lincoln, was an owner of Redhall. He was a person of some consequence, because on at least one occasion he was in the retinue of Alexander III when he was travelling in England. On one of these journeys, however, William blotted his copybook by poaching venison in Sherwood Forest and only an earnest plea in 1261 from his royal master saved him from the ire of the English king whose forest laws he had recklessly broken.

It is not known whether William le Grant himself built the Castle of Rubea Aula – Redhall – high on a promontory above the Dell, but it is written that he granted the lands of Redhall to Sir Alexander de Meyners, born about the year 1235. The northern corruption of his name to Menzies has survived to this day.

Sir Alexander was not only a local baron, but a politician. When Alexander III fell to his death over the cliffs at Kinghorn in 1286, leaving Margaret, his three year old grand-daughter, in Norway as Queen of Scotland, de Meyners of Redhall attended the Parliament meetings south of the Border at which the marriage of the child-queen to the English Prince Edward was discussed. When the startling news came from the north that the young queen had died in Orkney on her journey from Norway to her Scottish kingdom, English envoys stayed at Redhall during the crisis.

Sir Alexander's troubles began when he opposed the attempt by King Edward I, Hammer of the Scots, to put Balliol on the throne of Scotland, and he was captured at Dunbar on 28th April 1296 and taken to the Tower of London. From there Sir Alexander was forced to go to Flanders to fight for the English king, and he also had to raise a fighting band to go with him. Did his Colinton vassals have to go? If so, this was surely the first of many times in the history of Colinton that its men were conscripted for service abroad.

In the circumstances, the Hammer of the Scots can hardly have received much of a welcome when, after defeating Wallace at the Battle of Falkirk, he arrived at Redhall in 1298. Natural resentment apart, the harvest was ripe and the Colinton families had little time to do any mandatory hunting and waiting on a foreign king. This was a very bad year of famine in Scotland and they needed all their energies to provide for their own families.

Baron Redhall, however, had a proud end to his story. He escaped from England and fought with Robert the Bruce at Bannockburn, for which service he was made an earl. Doubtless many of his Colinton vassals had to go to Bannockburn and fight with him, but although this great victory must have cheered them, it did little to improve the lot of their families at home. It was still a battle to cut the peats, to grow enough food, and to keep the elements out of the dark turf-roofed cot-houses in which they lived. It was also still a struggle to resist disease, and when, in 1350, the Black Death came to Scotland, the people of Colinton had as little hope of survival as anyone else.

Andrew de Wyntoun, in his 14th century chronicle, says it all:

> *In Scotland the first Pestilence*
> *Began, of so great violence*
> *That it was said, of living men*
> *The third part it destroyed then;*
> *After that within Scotland*
> *A year or more it was wedand*   *wedand* = raging
> *Before that time was never seen*
> *A pestilence in our land so keen;*
> *Both men, and bairnies, and women,*
> *It spared not for to kill them.*

There was often no time for shriving, often no time for burying. The bodies of the victims lay out in the bracken, where they had been dragged by those in the family who were left with enough strength to do so. If ever there was a time when the priest of Ethelred's church had to justify his existence, it was then.

The *Registrum de Dunfermlyne* gives the first known name of a vicar of Hailes as Richard de Moravia in 1226. Richard's forebears were probably the Flemish family of Freskin, who arrived in West Lothian during the reign of David I. Upon receiving grants of land in Moray, the Freskins took the name of de Moravia.

Richard was possibly still in office when his bishop came with so much panoply to consecrate the church. He seems to have been quite an aggressive person, but in fairness to him his legal actions were all in defence of the possessions of his church. Not only did he have a dispute with Thomas of Restalrig about the boundary at the Hole Mill (already mentioned) but he also had the temerity to argue with the Abbot of Holyrood about the teinds of the 'Craggis de Gorgin', now the Craiglockhart Hills. The matter was settled out of court, with Vicar Richard withdrawing his suit and the Abbot of Holyrood agreeing to give the Church of St Cuthbert of Hailes an annual sum of two shillings for candles.

Vicar Richard's third dispute was with the Brothers of the Hospital of St Leonard in Edinburgh about the tithes of the Mill of Dregern, and again he was fobbed off with candles for Pentecost and Martinmas. (Here we see an early reference in the parish to the name Dreghorn, which may be derived from the Gaelic *Tre-quern*, meaning the 'farm-town by the swamp or by the alder trees'.) From these records it can be learned, therefore, that Vicar Richard not only had a well-lit church, but that some of his parishioners were mill workers. As early as the thirteenth century there were two mills working on the Water of Leith – Hole Mill in the Dell, and Dreghorn Mill on the Bonaly or Redford Burn at Dreghorn.

The next recorded vicar was William de Camera in 1378, who was described in a papal bull as 'nobly born and a student of canon law'. The papal letter of Clement VII of Avignon about William, addressed to 'the official of Paris', requested a mandate to provide William de Camera, MA, vicar of the parish of Halys, in the St Andrews diocese, to a canonry of Moray with expectation of a prebend, which was a share of the revenues. If William was nobly born and had studied the law in Paris, it is unlikely that he would have been content to live in a meagre lean-to hut at the church at Hailes – perhaps he had the first well-appointed manse in the parish. He clearly was an ambitious man, because he moved on to be clerk of the Aberdeen diocese and he was the subject of more papal letters, and apparently some dispute. Clement VII finally wrote:

> *This is a declaration to put an end to all doubt in the matter, that William de Camera, senior, M.A., Clerk of Aberdeen diocese, who is of noble birth and studied canon law at Paris for several years, was a member of the pope's household at the time of his provision to a canonry of Dunkeld.*

Study in Paris seems to have been quite common for priests, for a successor of William de Camera is referred to in papal letters as having taught there. Richard Hunter, who came to the parish in 1394, lectured on canon law for four years in Paris before returning to take up positions which suggest a certain amount of plurality – he was vicar of Hailes and 'provided to a canonry of Dunkeld with expectation of a prebend'. It is interesting that the church at Hailes had again a connection with Dunkeld, the abbacy of its founder, Ethelred.

On the death of Richard Hunter, there is recorded the papal appointment of John de Carrike who apparently came into this life with the 'defect of birth as the son of a religious priest and an unmarried woman'. Pope Benedict XIII graciously 'dispensed' John of this blemish, and said that he must be promoted to holy orders and permitted to hold a benefice in the parish church of Halys, St Andrews diocese, value not exceeding 18 pounds sterling to a non-resident. John died after five years in office at Hailes, and the parish was taken over by Vicar Nicholas Chylde, who came from the Dunkeld diocese.

The value of the benefice had now gone up to 22 pounds and Vicar Nicholas must have been grateful for his good fortune – he had been within a whisker of being thrown out of the Church for backing the wrong Pope at the time when two prelates claimed the papacy, one in Avignon and one in Rome. A letter in 1419 to Pope Michael revealed Nicholas's anxiety. It stated that because of his miscalculation, he 'fears that he may be molested in future' and 'supplicates that the Pope would ratify the foregoing with all the consequences and provide him anew to the said parish church, whether void as above or howsoever, notwithstanding his adhesion to Peter de Luna before his rejection by the realm of Scotland'. (Peter de Luna, who had been Benedict XIII, was deposed from the papacy in 1419.)

This was a traumatic time in Scottish history, for in the interminable skirmishing with the English, the Scottish king, James I, was captured and could not return for 18 years. Later he met the fate of so many of his predecessors – he was assassinated. In the chaos that followed, the barons ruled; but though justice became fragmented, changes of land use were still carefully recorded. Therefore it was minuted that the lands of Oxgangs, Hailes and Redhall changed hands, and that the accounts of the Chamberlain of Scotland at the Exchequer in 1438 showed for Redhall figures for the 'Lands of Colytoun, Dreggarn, Banale, Wodal and the tenandry of Foslane at Colytoun'.

Ownership of rights also changed in the church at Hailes. By the time Vicar James Gray was appointed in 1491, the superiority of the Church had been taken away from Holyrood and conferred on the Canons of St Anthony of Leith by Bishop Kennedy of St Andrews in 1445. Their Preceptory was built in St Anthony's Wynd, an alley off the Kirkgate, and there was a splendid church and burying ground. To this Preceptory was also granted the greater teinds of the lands of Redhall, Oxgangs, Colinton and half of Comiston, as well as the vicarage teinds of the whole of the parish. The monks of Dunfermline managed to keep the remainder of the teinds, however, and the business traffic to and fro between Hailes and Dunfermline continued until the Reformation. The spiritual help that came to Colinton, in return for produce and stock for the monks, was always very much needed, but seldom more so than in 1498 when Vicar James Gray found himself in an area direly affected by disease. So concerned was the Town Council of Edinburgh about this 'wame ill', that it forbad – on pain of death – the people of Hailes, together with their produce, entering the town without first being decontaminated in the 'rynnand Water of Leith'. They also had to disinfect their houses with burning heather.

By the end of the fifteenth century, therefore, Hailes had a well-established identity. It was no longer a few scattered settlements along the river and up on the Pentlands, almost without a name. As a result of the establishment of Ethelred's church, Hailes had become a place in regular contact with the seat of government; it was in the forefront of the Romanisation of the Scottish Church; it was enmeshed firmly in the red tape of Rome and, because the Church and the feudal system flourished together, it found itself, however reluctantly, involved with the politics of the age. The people of Hailes now had to accept that, in times of war, their men would be conscripted for baronial service and their women would have to try to get the flax harvest in on their own.

CHAPTER 3

Stands of Armour for the Colinton Men

THE people of Hailes now had a sense of place. There were mills on the Water of Leith for waulking cloth and grinding grain, and the farming system which had evolved encouraged people to live near each other. The men had also learned how to ditch and drain land, and the bog below Redhall and the marshes round about were therefore made into good pasture and firm ground for cot-houses. The isolated settlements, which had previously been dispersed over a large area, started to huddle together in the valley of the Dell, with the ford at the foot of what was to become Spylaw Street, the focal point of the village.

The name of Hailes itself had also changed over the centuries. The first surviving reference to it in the confirmation of David I of his brother's gift around 1128, is by the Latin name of Hale. Over the years this varied in documents to Halis, Haillis, Hailles, Haills and Hailes. The scribes when copying out documents liked

to have an individuality of their own. In all the variations, though, the root remains. It is from the Old English *halh*, meaning a nook or a haugh, or, as stated in E Ekwall's *Concise Dictionary of English Place-Names*, 'the land in a corner formed by a bend' – a name tailor-made for the curve of the Water of Leith in the Dell.

At some point over the years, however, one of those with a close association to the parish of Hailes was a man called Colban, a Gaelicised version of the Old Norse name Kolbeinn. As the Vikings had rampaged down from the North, they had implanted far and wide names from their language.

Colban must have been a man of character or stature in the community. The ninth Comes (or Earl) of Fife who, like Prince Ethelred before him, had vast tracts of hunting land in the vicinity, was called Colban. Or perhaps there was a tacksman, a feuar, with this name, or perhaps the land in the centre of the settlement was worked by a Colban. In any event, for whatever reason, the people, with their new sense of place, began to call their village 'Colban's farm' or 'Colban's toun'.

The *Registrum Magni Sigilli Regum Scotorum* – the Great Seal – refers to Colbanestoun in 1319 and Colbanystone in 1406. The Acts of the Lords Auditors of Causes and Complaints shorten it to Colbantoun in 1479, and in the Acts of the Lords of Council in Civil Causes it became Colintoun in 1488. By the 17th century the spelling of the village's name had been varied to Collintoun, Collingtoun and a Latinised version of Colintona, but from then on the most common version was Colinton (though as late as 1739 the parish was officially known as 'Hales alias Collintoun').

Inextricably bound with the shift of emphasis from the ecclesiastical Lands of Hailes to the geographical area of the ford at the Dell and to the name of Colinton, was the rise of one family who were going to figure largely in Colinton's story. A glance at the memorial tablets in the vestibule of today's church confirms this. In 1529 some of the lands of Redhall – an area described as 'the lands and toun of Colintoun' – were hived off and sold to Mr James Foulis and his wife who came from Perthshire.

Some sources state that the Foulis were a Norman family who had come over to England with William the Conqueror and had moved north in search of land in the time of Malcolm Canmore's reign. It is asserted that they still used for their armorial bearing three laurel leaves, called 'feuilles' in their native Norman dialect, which gave them the name of Foulis. The Revd A W Cornelius Hallen, on the other hand, claims in his introduction to the *Account Book of Sir John Foulis of Ravelston*, that armorial bearings were unknown till many years after the Norman Conquest, and that records of the Foulis family did not appear until a mention of a burgess of Edinburgh called James Foulis in the fifteenth century. (At some point however, the family certainly did adopt armorial bearings with three laurel leaves – they are clearly depicted on the 1630 sundial of Sir James Foulis now on the church wall.)

Other barons in the area were important enough in their own way, but as with them all, their fortunes were as fickle as their politics. The third Lord Crichton of Hailes threw in his lot with the opponents of James III, and as a consequence forfeited his lands. These reverted back to the Abbey of Dunfermline. Redhall had difficulty meeting his obligations and sold off Woodhall and Bonaly to the laird of Cunynghamehead; Cunynghame was not popular for occupying and manuring a third part of those lands which actually belonged to the widow of his predecessor. William Wallace of Bonaly, no doubt with many of his Colinton men, was killed at Flodden, and Glencairn of Redhall subsequently became involved with the ensuing battles over the supremacy of the child king who inherited the throne after that national disaster.

It was a royal decree that barons, as part of their contract with the king for their land, had to keep at the ready so many stands of armour according to the size of their estate. They had to answer a call to arms with their knights and men and fight for at least forty days. If they failed to do so, the charter for their land was made null and void. Therefore, if they opted for the opposition, they took grave risks of dispossession.

In the Norman system favoured by David I, the lowest people in the pyramid of power to the king were the baron's serfs and in Colinton, as elsewhere, when a feudal baron built his castle, many of the people lost a measure of the freedom they had had under a Celtic regime. Whilst some were fortunate enough to be allowed to continue paying their 'cain and conveth' – their obligatory contribution of food – to a Norman overlord, just as they had done to a Celtic one, others came under a feudal sway which was so repressive that it was tantamount to slavery. They were forced to work without any pay on the baron's demesne – the 'Mains' – and they were not allowed to move away. They even had to get permission from their lord for the marriages of their daughters. Both the barons of Redhall and of Colinton would follow Norman customs encouraged by the king – it strengthened personal power.

From the outset, the Foulis family was purposeful, and as soon as the land purchase was through they set about establishing themselves in some style in the area. They had their Mains farm at Colinton Mains, and it can be presumed that they built themselves a dwelling of some kind as soon as they arrived in the area. However, as they acquired more and more land – Wester Swanston and Oxgangs in 1538, then Dreghorn, part of Bonaly, Baads and Pilmuir, mills on the river and some of the lands of Comiston – they ceased to be incomers and became the local landed gentry.

Clearly enjoying royal approval, they received in 1540 from James V a Crown Charter which incorporated all their lands into the Barony of Colinton and which laid down that *'domum super terris de Colintoun edificandam'* (the house required to be built on the lands of Colinton) should be the main dwelling house of the barony. Mr James Foulis had become the first Baron of Colinton, and he now embarked upon building his stately home – Colinton Castle, whose ivy-covered ruin still stands towering over the headmaster's house in the grounds of what is now Merchiston Castle School.

Built of red stone quarried locally across the river at Redhall Quarry, the Castle was designed on an L-plan. It had a splendid location, not only from the point of view of defence, but of amenity. It stood high on the east bank of the Water of Leith, commanding the valley below. To the north-east could be seen the craggy rock of Edinburgh Castle, and to the south were the Pentlands. On the ground floor it had small arched windows, some arrow slits for defence, cellarage space with vaulted ceilings

COLINTON CASTLE, BUILT BY SIR JAMES FOULIS.

and a stair in the angle of the L-shape. On its walls the masons' marks of the builders can still be seen.

Over the years it was altered and enlarged – at the beginning of the seventeenth century a second stair tower was added – but even in its simpler original form it must have been awe-inspiring for the families below in the Dell. A steep bridle path led down to the ford, and the bases of some gateposts can still be seen in the Castle grounds indicating its route. These gateposts give the headmaster's house its present name of Castle Gates.

The first Baron Colinton was heavily involved in politics. He had married Katherine Brown, cousin of Sir Adam Otterburn of Redhall, and Otterburn was to be a colleague in the law courts, a relative by marriage, and of course a neighbour. Together, they were among the Commissioners appointed by the Scottish Parliament to try to achieve some peace by negotiating a marriage between the infant Mary Queen of Scots and Prince Edward of England. How history would have changed if Otterburn of Redhall and Foulis of Colinton had, with their colleagues, achieved an engagement that lasted between those two young royal children.

The second Baron Colinton – also James – decided it would be best to support young James VI after the ill-advised flight of Mary Queen of Scots to England, and the third baron very nearly came to grief when he joined the conspiracy known as the Raid of Ruthven, a plan to kidnap the boy king and thereby oust the power of those controlling him.

This Baron Colinton recovered himself well, however. He was astute enough to marry the girl next door, Agnes Heriot of Lymphoy, who did not come to the marriage empty-handed. She brought feu rights of land as far afield as Glasgow, which enabled James, with some judicious exchanging of charters, to acquire more land nearer home – Bonaly, Oxgangs, Auchingane, and also Little Fordel and Kirkslope which were both adjacent to Dreghorn.

When Agnes died in 1593, her testament recorded that they had on the Lands of Colinton 34 oxen, 117 sheep, 19 calves, horses, two mares, and many other domestic animals. On the farm they grew oats, wheat, pease and bere, and they had a well-stocked barn against the winter. Up at Dreghorn they clearly used the Pentlands for pasture, for they had 260 sheep and 146 lambs. In addition there were 17 oxen for the ploughing, 68 hogs and again a farmyard full of other animals. They sowed the same crops as at Colinton Mains, and filled the barn with wheat.

Whether this was a happy marriage is impossible to say, but certainly James wished posterity to know that he thought well of Agnes. At her death he had her grave marked thus: *Heir Lyes Ane Honourable Woman A. Hiriot Spous to J. Foulis of Collingtoun vas qvha died 8 August 1593.*

This 400 year old tablet was put in the Foulis family burial vault across the Water of Leith, below the home where Agnes raised five sons. The oldest surviving inscription in today's church, it is now embedded in the wall of the South Aisle. It links present-day worshippers with a local lady who remembered when Henry VIII invaded Scotland in 1542, who smelled Edinburgh burning after the Earl of Hertford's invasion in 1544, and who wondered what the world was coming to when word seeped over the Channel of the new ideas on the Christian faith of Martin Luther and John Calvin. And that fiery John Knox, banging his pulpit in St John's Church in Perth, going round the country talking of a Reformed Kirk – what was *he* up to?

CHAPTER 4

Testing Times

NO ONE in Scotland escaped the trauma of the Reformation, and the Colinton villagers, like everyone else, found themselves torn apart by creeds and by dogma. They had been brought up to believe that if they did not worship according to the Roman Catholic rites of the vicar of Hailes, they would go to hell. Now they were being told that they would go to hell if they did.

To the thinking men and women of the village, the crisis in the Church came as no surprise. The Roman Catholic Church in Scotland had been in decline for some time. Pluralities for kings' kinsmen and bargaining counters for land deals, many church benefices had become so removed from the Word of God that their inconsistencies were glaring to all. Thus, when Sir Andrew Binning succeeded Mr Robert Lyndesay as vicar – his title of 'Sir' was a traditional church one for those who had not aspired to a Master's degree which held the title of Magister – he came to a church that was in the Diocese of St Andrews, a rural deanery of Linlithgow, with parsonage to Dunfermline Abbey and vicarage to the Hospital of St Anthony in Leith. The Colinton pennies in the plate had to stretch far. The last person, however, to become wealthy would be Vicar Andrew, who, with his comparatively simple lifestyle, would have a job to quell the serious sin of envy when he bowed to his superior bishops and abbots, plump with their rich living, and dressed in the fine robes which the benefices of the village churches such as his provided.

In the confusion of those Reformation times it is not clear how long Sir Andrew hung on to his job at Hailes. In his testament in the Register of the Privy Council he is described as late as 1575 as 'Sir Andrew Bynning, vicar of the Kirk at the Brig of

Hailes'. Yet post Reformation records list Alexander Forrester as Reader in charge in 1567, followed by the Revd John Durie who was minister in 1569. John Blak and Andrew Robesoun filled in as Readers when the pulpit was empty. The next minister in 1574 was the Revd Adam Lichtone, who, such was the shortage of ministers in the Reformed Church, had the linked charge of Currie, Hailes and St Catherines in the Hopes, which is now submerged under Glencorse Reservoir.

It would be good to think that Sir Andrew Binning was allowed to remain in peaceful retirement somewhere in the parish. After the Reformation there was some prosecution of 'mass mongers', but legally there was no penalty for refusing to work in the Reformed Church. In addition, the financial structure of the Roman Catholic Church was not swept away overnight, so that there was still a system for Sir Andrew to get a stipend to live on. This also meant that it was perfectly legal for him to continue to be styled 'Vicar of the Church of Hailes', as he was in his testament.

When he died he was not destitute by any means, for it is recorded that he left a sideboard with two folding leaves, a feather bed with a bolster and a pair of pillows, a 'meikle kist', four great tin plates, various other trenchers and dishes, and a respectable array of furniture. He had several pairs of sheets, pairs of blankets and a bed-cover. In his kists were three 'great law books', a worsted gown lined with fur, another short gown of worsted and a new grey cloak.

He must have cut a colourful dash in the village, because he went about wearing a 'side coitt of collor de roy' – *ie* a purple greatcoat. In addition he had a blue one which he wore with white doublets, white stockings, linen shirts, and a black hat. He also had a crook.

His flock, however, had changed their ways. By 1560, when the Scottish Reformation

Parliament passed its measures, all traces of the Roman form of worship had to be removed from the parish churches. All links with Rome were cut off, no mass could be said, and Romish church furniture and relics were removed from services. When the people of Colinton went to church, they now found that the altar had gone, there were no Stations of the Cross, no incense and no crucifix. The church, stripped of its Roman splendour, had become a very plain building indeed. It was also at this time in England that there disappeared from Durham Cathedral the famous Black Rood of Scotland, Queen Margaret's reliquary, which she and all her family, including Ethelred, had worshipped, and which she was holding when she died.

During all the Reformation struggles, the local barons in Colinton continued to be involved with affairs of state. Thus it was that when five of the Scottish nobility, fired by a zeal for Protestantism, formed the 'First Band' of what was to be known as the 'Lords of the Congregation', a signatory was Glencairn, who still had a feudal superiority over parts of the Barony of Redhall. This stand in 1557, which was not, it must be said, wholly divorced from the realisation that there would be economic and political gain in breaking up the Roman Catholic Church's grip on the land, was a pledge to strive for the reformation of the Church:

> *To apply our whole power, substance, and our very lives, to maintain, set forward, and establish the most blessed word of God* [and to] *labour at our possibility to have faithful Ministers purely and truly to minister Christ's Evangel and Sacraments to his people.*

These were the brave words of Glencairn's covenant, which was to be the forerunner of the National Covenant in eighty years' time. The text must have been read with foreboding by Vicar Andrew Binning in his study at Colinton.

After the impact of the covenant of the First Band, events in the country began to move fast. John Knox took a ship back to Scotland from his refuge on the Continent, where he had absorbed much from the Protestant doctrines of John Calvin. He was in the capital to provide a not-too-welcoming committee for his newly-widowed Roman Catholic sovereign, Mary Queen of Scots, when she returned from France two years later. At home in Colinton, William Cunynghame of Woodhall was quick to throw in his lot with the reforming clergy, and he was one of those sent by the Lords of the Congregation to demand liberty of conscience from Queen Mary. He also attended the Reformation Parliament of 1560, and signed John Knox's Bond supporting the reformed religion. There can be little doubt that the Colinton families farming the Woodhall Lands and working in the waulk-mills and corn mills which were now there, had to lose quickly any nostalgia that they might have had for the old faith.

John Cunynghame, William's son, played an even more dangerous game than his father, when he became implicated in the murder of the Queen's favourite, Rizzio. With Protestant protection, however, he survived with his lands intact, and had the satisfaction of seeing Hailes' first Protestant minister, the Revd John Durie, installed in 1569. No doubt another cause for celebration for John Cunynghame, sitting in his fine tower in Woodhall in 1587, would be the execution of Mary Queen of Scots at Fotheringay. But for those in the village, this was no clear signal of the end of confusion in their parish church. Protestantism may have been established – but what type of Protestantism was it finally to be, Presbyterian or Episcopalian?

In all the plotting and planning of Church and State since the days of the flight of Mary Queen of Scots, however, daily life was still just as influenced by factors like the weather as matters spiritual. This was a time of bad weather and poor harvests. Indeed, times were so desperate that when the younger Laird of Redhall was on the roll of the Justices of the Peace for Edinburgh, it was decided that 'they could not gudlie put in execution' the harsh repressions required by the law against the beggars and the maimed. There was so much sickness and famine that the poor people could hardly transport themselves from one parish to the next, and it was therefore decreed by the Privy Council, with rare compassion for the times, that every parish and every landed gentleman within every parish had to 'interteine his awin pure'.

There was no mercy, however, for the farmers trying to get their produce to market in the midst of the strife raging between the supporters of Queen Mary and those of her son James – the Queensmen and the Kingsmen – and for the people of Colinton, so near to the hub of events, things were particularly difficult. While the Queen's party held Edinburgh Castle together with the Niddries and places to the west, 'the Regent and the kingis favouraris stuffit the houssis of Craigmillar, Merchingstoun, Sclatfurd, Reidhall, Corstorphine and the College thairof, and the Abbey with all places about the town of Edinburgh'.

One of the tactics of the Kingsmen was to starve out their opponents in the centre of Edinburgh; to do this in 1572 they threw a blockade round the town, and with brute force prevented all meat, drink, fuel and other necessities from being sent in. As is usual in such a strategy, the people at the bottom of the pyramid of power suffered most, and the folk of Colinton were harried beyond endurance by the men who had garrisoned themselves at Redhall. They arrested some poor farmers who were trying to get their sheep and corn to market, and, as an impressive deterrent to others, they hanged two of them and branded the others on the cheek.

However, the villagers were so needful for victuals that the next day five women attempted the journey with the carts. There was no quarter given to them either. One was executed by drowning – history does not relate how this poor victim was selected out of the five – and the remaining four were whipped and branded.

In the face of these atrocities and crippling poverty, it must have been hard for the people of Colinton to accept the edict of the Statutory Act in 1572 which laid down that all of the Reformed clergy had to have a manse and four acres of arable glebe. Was it out of the frying pan and into the fire? Had they not just shaken themselves free of the demands of the Roman Church, now to find that the minister of their new church was to get a fine house and more land for farming than they could ever hope for? Where was this glebe to be? By the ford? In the best farming land of the village?

The problem was not immediate, because ministers in the fledgling Protestant Church were still in very short supply. The Revd John Hall, when he was inducted to Colinton in 1579, must, however, have looked for his proper accommodation, and the congregation now found themselves under the strict guidelines of the Second Book of Discipline which held them in a grip just as tight as that of the Roman Catholic Church.

A 1622 WINDOW AT BABERTON HOUSE

They found for instance that they could not leave the parish without a 'Testificate', a document from the minister stating whether a person was of good moral standing. The ways they had to worship the Lord were laid down as harshly as ever and the rule of the elders was to become so vindictive and merciless that it is difficult to associate it with the compassion of their Master.

Officially, the elders' function was to maintain godly discipline, and to fulfil the social and ecclesiastical functions placed upon the parish. Their disciplinary remit thus covered all aspects of Sabbath observance and undesirable behaviour, such as drunkenness and sexual irregularity. In practice, they frequently acted as judges and Sabbath spies, sentencing their neighbours to months on end of punishment at the repentance pillar, seemingly with little regard for any extenuating circumstances. The Kirk Session minutes are an unhappy catalogue of such happenings. The village girl raped by the young laird in the barley field had no chance of sympathy for herself or her unborn child.

On the plus side, however, the Reformation was to bring the people education. The Revd Peter Hewat, who was called to be minister of Colinton in 1596, has an 'MA' after his name and might have studied at St Andrews, or the brand new university in Edinburgh. The people of the village had a chance to be educated too. The creators of the Book of Discipline laid down that the minister was to be elected by the congregation. In order to do this, the members of the congregation could not be ignorant. 'Godliness was the true foundation of all learning.' Let there be parish schools. The scheme was excellent, except that it was considered unnecessary to provide higher education for girls. The miracle is that, in those days, when still burned women as witches, that they thought that girls should be educated at all.

There is no record of a parish school building in Colinton before the one in the out-house 'at the minister's yett' near the present church, but the children were at first taught in the church. The boys, if they were 'docile', that is teachable, were then sent down to the university in the town. Teaching in the church ended in 1663 when the elders were displeased at the way the children were vandalising the pews. As in the church, so in the schools there was to be no slacking, and the progress of the pupils was tested every quarter by the minister and the elders. It is to be hoped that they, in their turn, had been sufficiently educated to undertake this task. Education was not meant to be fun, and above the door of the first school building was carved the strict injunction *Aut doce, aut disce, aut abi'* – either teach, or learn, or go away. If the children had anything so frivolous as play-time, they may have played 'tig' around the yew tree which had been planted near the manse about thirty years previously – the same yew tree which was to become a pirate's lookout for Robert Louis Stevenson some two centuries later and bear a swing for the ministers' children of more recent times.

While the edicts of the Church were forward-looking, there was still a feudal framework in Scotland. When Revd John Hall was minister at the Hailes church, he found that his sovereign, James VI, who had conveniently ruled that the lands dispossessed from the Roman Catholic Church by the Reformation now belonged to the Crown, annexed the superiority of Hailes.

This was a moment of history for the church at Hailes, because it marked the beginning of the severance of the link between Hailes and the monks of Dunfermline, a connection which had lasted nearly five hundred years since the days of Prince Ethelred. The move, however, was merely to transfer superiority from the abbey to lay ownership. The king rewarded John Hay, a clerk of the Lord of Council and Session, with the lands of the Preceptory of St Anthony at Leith and the church lands of Hailes with the teinds of the parish. In return, Mr Hay had to pay the minister part of his stipend.

Others to benefit at the expense of the people of Hailes were the Earl of Dunfermline and Sir John Maitland, founder of the Lauderdale family, who were in turn given the patronage of the parish. The earl, however, seemed to be somewhat cavalier about his responsibilities, for he refused to pay his share of the stipend for the minister, the Revd James Thomson, until finally in 1608 poor Mr Thomson had to abandon the parish in search of a square meal. In consequence, the Presbytery of Edinburgh made an impassioned plea to the king to 'cause see out some meane, that a congregation so neere to Edinburghe, served ever since the reformation of religion, be not displanted by the evill will of evill meaning men'.

Either this appeal was successful, or other local patronage provided the cash for the stipend, for Mr Thomson was persuaded to return. He died still minister of the parish in 1635. During his time he saw many changes. While the connection of the Glencairns with Redhall waned after two hundred years, the fortunes of the Foulis family waxed more strongly than ever. Mr Thomson's neighbours up at Colinton Castle were empire building at great speed, acquiring more and more land in the parish. In addition, the Foulis cousins of Ravelston were taking over Craiglockhart. The parish boundary was also changed at this time, for in 1630 the lands of Craiglockhart were disjoined from their ancient parish church of St Cuthbert's-by-the-Castle, and added to the parish of Colinton, 'for the convenience of the worshippers'.

For the people of Colinton, however, alterations of bound

aries and big land deals did not bring much change to their daily lives. While Mr Thomson sat in his manse writing sermons, or walked about his parish, he heard the clatter of the many mills up and down the Water of Leith grinding corn or waulking, just as they had for centuries. Unchanged, too, was the click of the girls' distaffs and spindles, as they sat in their thatched cottages spinning wool. When he smelled the aromas of the cooking pots, Mr Thomson could guess with accuracy what his parishioners were having to eat – their diet was still limited.

There were as yet no potatoes, turnips, tea or coffee in the district, but from their oats they got oatmeal which made porridge, oatcakes and brose, from barley they got ale, and from the cows' milk they got crowdie, cheese and butter. For special occasions they toasted him in Atholl brose – a brose of oatmeal, whisky and honey – and had a cream crowdie made of toasted oatmeal and whipped cream. But special occasions were few and far between. By the time the barons and feudal superiors had exacted their dues, there was only a meagre existence left for the village people.

Thirlage still flourished – the enforced use by the tenants of the estate owner's mill and the consequent abuses and profits which such a monopoly encouraged. In addition the people still had to submit to the bullying of the tacksman who collected their master's rents. Many was the argument about the tenth sheaf, which the tacksman made sure was not the smallest, and much was the anguish when advantage of good weather could not be taken for ricking the crops until the collector had been. There was no security of tenure and beggary was the option when a family was turned out of its dwelling.

Not even the new ways of worshipping in the village church were safe. The people had just got used to the reformed services and the rule of the Presbytery when in 1610 Episcopacy was restored in Scotland. For the next eighty years there were to be reversals to Presbyterianism, compromises and controversies so that from one month to the next the people hardly knew what form of service they were to receive each Sunday.

It must have been equally confusing for Mr Thomson, but on the 5th March 1634, he made a brave stand, refusing to conform to the instructions of his bishop regarding the method of celebrating Communion – did he and the Colinton people baulk at kneeling for the sacrament? He was not expelled from the Church, however, and was still minister of the parish when he died a year later. He left a widow, Helen, who after nine years was admitted 'as ane ordinar pensioner by the Session of Edinburgh, to receive quarterly the sume of 20 merkis'. For the Thomsons' successor in the manse, however, there were to be even more difficult times.

CHAPTER 5

Cromwell Comes to Colinton

THE morning of August 18th 1650, dawned as any other that summer in Colinton. It had been an exceptionally wet month, and there must have been worry about the harvest, but the clinkum-clankum of the waulking went on at Boag's Mill as usual, and there was some grain to be ground at Davies' Mill, at Jinkabout, and at the Hole Mill behind the manse. Inside the thatched stone cottages, the women and girls got on with their chores, but as in the smithy, in the fields and in the mills, the talk was as ever about the Roundheads.

Cromwell's troops, since their victory at the Battle of Preston, had been camping at Galachlaw, just east of Fairmilehead. They were getting more and more hungry. Their Scots opponent, General Leslie, in his delaying tactics, employed a scorched earth policy which left little in the countryside for the English soldiers to commandeer. More than once Cromwell had had to withdraw his troops to Musselburgh, where his supplies were coming in by sea from England. On the 6th August, however, the seas were so high that the boats could not get in, and he had marched the wretched men back once again to Dunbar to try to provision them there. The casualties during this operation were enormous. Not only were his men being constantly harried by Scots guerrilla troops in the hills between Galachlaw and the coast, but because of the bad weather, hunger and disease, he had 2000 troops on the sick list at Galachlaw alone.

When the men had withdrawn from Galachlaw, there was quiet rejoicing among the Colinton people, but their relief was short-lived. On the 18th August the cry went up in the hills and fields – a column of Roundheads could be seen marching back.

Bent on finding food, driving north, and revenging the Royalist stand of the local lairds – *ie* Sir James Foulis of Colinton, and Hamilton of Redhall – ten companies of General Monck's regiment under the command of Captain Gough and Captain Holms, stormed into the village. No cottage had a bar on the door strong enough to resist them. The effect not only on the fortunes of the lairds, but of the ordinary people was to be profound.

The contemporary account of John Nicoll, who wrote a diary about the events between 1650 and 1667, describes graphically the events which followed:

Upon Settirday, the 24th August 1650, our armuy resavit a great disgrace in this manner; to wit, General Cromwell and his airmy haifing past throw this Kingdom fra Berwik to the place of Collintoun, without any opposition maid by ony of the gentillmenis houssis by the way quhair they past, untill they come to the hous of Reidhall, within thrie myles by west Edinburgh; in the quhilk house of Reidhall, the Laird of Reidhall with thrie scoir sodgeris lay, with provisioun, and keipit and defendit the hous aganes the Englisches, and galled his sodgeris, and pat thame bak severall tymes with the los of sindry sodgeris.

> *The Englische Generall, taking this very grevouslie, that such a waik hous sould hald out againes him, and be ane impedimeng in his way, he and his airmuy lying so neir unto it; thairfoir, he causit draw his cannoun to the hous, and thair, fra four hoiuris in the morning till ten in the foirnune that day, he causit the cannoun to play on his hous, encampit a great number of his sodgeris about it, with pik and musket, bot all to lytill purpos; for the Laird and the pepill in the hous defendit valientlie ever till their powder failled; and eftir it failled they did not give over, evir luiking for help fra owr ain airmy, qhua wes then lying at Corstorphyn, within thrie quarteris of any muyle to the house; of quhais help thai war disapoynted.*
>
> *General Cromwell perceaving thair power to be gone, and that no assistance wes gevin thame, he causit pittardis* [explosives] *to be brocht to the hous, quhairwith he blew up the dures, enterit the hous at dures and windois, and eftir slaughter on both sydes (bot much moir to the Englisches then the Scottis) tuik all that wer in the hous prissoners, tirred thame naked, seased on all the money and guidis that wer thairin, quhilk wes much, be ressoun that sindry gentillmen about haid put thair guidis thair for saiftie.*
>
> *So this hous and pepill thairin wer takin in the sicht and face of our airmy, quha thocht it dangerous to hazard thameselffis in such ane expeditioun, the eneymie haiffing the advantage of the ground and hillis about him for his defence.*

Cromwell, however, had a grudging admiration for his stubborn adversary at Redhall, because shortly afterwards he gave him his liberty – and presumably his clothes – commending much 'his valour and activitie for holding out so stoutlie againes him that hous of Reidhall'.

Redhall's neighbour at Colinton Castle did not fare so well. Foulis, firmly backing the Royalist cause, had at the time of the Battle of Preston levied at his own expense a regiment of horse which cost him £6600 Scots. From then on his losses in men and goods were so great that his family's fortunes never recovered.

Without much struggle, Cromwell's troops stormed Colinton Castle and proceeded to burn and loot on Foulis' land throughout the entire neighbourhood. From firing and ransacking the Castle

– the roof was burnt, the doors and windows smashed and all the furnishings plundered – they went on to destroy all the tenants' houses, the barns, the byres and the crops between Colinton village and Bowbridge beyond Swanston.

The home farm at Colinton Mains was particularly badly hit – all the corn and stock were pillaged by the hungry soldiers. It is not difficult to imagine the suffering of the cottar folk during this invasion, when so many lives were lost, breadwinners maimed, homes burnt and food stolen.

Foulis himself managed to escape, but not for long. In the following year he was taken. He had gone north to Alyth to attend a meeting of the Estates and he paid dearly for his diligence. Monck's troops, who were then besieging Dundee, heard of his whereabouts and captured him. He was sent by sea to London, where he spent many long years in captivity and was lucky to escape death. On his return to Scotland after the Restoration, some of his friends backed his claim to Parliament for losses amounting to £77,666 Scots, but the mere recording of this can have given him and his family little comfort. Swingeing debts were now to be the lot of the Foulis descendants so that in time they had to sell off the Colinton Estate bit by bit – Dreghorn, Comiston, Craiglockhart, and finally the Castle itself in 1801.

The restored king, however, did his best by Foulis in 1661. Charles II made Sir James a judge when the Court of Session was reopened – a profession to be followed by his son, who took the title of Lord Redford. When their lordships went off to court in their grand coaches, however, they passed through a land still devastated by the recent English incursions, and at home their workers were still broken and bewildered by recent events.

Even in their church there was confusion. The older people among them could recall the extraordinary occasion when their minister, the Revd William Ogston, was shamefully manhandled and bundled out of the parish in 1639 for deserting it 'twenty weeks togidder'. It must be remembered that this was a time when the Church swung between Presbyterianism and Episcopalianism, so no eyebrows had been raised when Mr Ogston had come to the parish on the recommendation of Bishop Forbes. But he proved to be too High Kirk for the people, for when he examined his flock before Communion to see if they were worthy of it, he, as instructed by his bishop at his ordination, required them to kneel. The people, accustomed to the Low Kirk ways of the last minister, Mr Thomson, were incensed, and many of them marched off to Currie Kirk or to other churches in Edinburgh where the ministers did not insist upon such idolatrous ways of worship.

Poor Mr Ogston, left with an empty church and a hostile parish, was branded a Papist and set upon by a mob of Edinburgh women who 'did showre him with strokes'. He compounded his troubles by refusing to sign the Covenant. Small wonder he deserted his flock.

At the time he must have been an object of pity, for he was not only deprived of a livelihood but his home. However, better times did come to him, at the expense of another minister. When the Restoration brought back Episcopacy, the incumbent of Corstorphine was in his turn thrown out for refusing to acknowledge the bishops, and Mr Ogston was called to that vacancy. It is doubtful whether he ever visited his neighbouring minister in Colinton, the Revd Thomas Garven, who had succeeded him.

In Mr Garven's time a great change came for the children of Colinton – they were *all* to receive education. Scotland had, of course, had schools for a long time: the 1496 Act required that the eldest sons and heirs of the barons and freeholders of substance be sent to school. In addition, at the time of the Reformation, the First Book of Discipline had enshrined the value of education: 'Seeing that God hath determined that his Church here in earth shall be taught not by angels but by men ....' But John Knox's Book of Reformation could only recommend, not legislate.

And in 1616 it was enacted 'that in everie parroche of this kingdome whair convenient

A DESPERATE SEARCH FOR A BAPTISM.

means may be had for interteyning a scoole, that a scoole sal be establisheit, and a fitt persone appointit to teache the same, upoun the expensis of the parochinnaris according to the quantitie and qualitie of the paroche ....'

A new act in 1646, however, placed firmly in the hands of the heritors – the landowners – of every parish the obligation to provide and maintain suitable schools. The boys and girls of Colinton were no longer free to herd flocks and spin wool for their parents all day; they were now expected to go to school.

There would not have been much school-work done on the 3rd September of 1650, however, when Cromwell achieved his devastating victory at Dunbar. Such was the fear and confusion in the village that even the new minister, Revd Alexander Livingstone, fled to Fife, and the school was to be shut for a year.

The earliest Kirk Session minutes are those of 7th August 1651. Presumably there were minutes previous to this, but there is no trace of any. It is feasible that they were destroyed by Cromwell's rampaging troops who have no record of respecting church property. Reference is, however, made to this time of destruction. Mr Livingstone, having deemed it safe to return to his parish, asked, 'If there was any scandal or notorious sin committed in the Parish during his late and sad absence (being for the space of twelve months of his abode in Fyfe after the lamentable loss and scattering of Dunbar, which fell upon the 3rd of September in 1650) to which answer was given of none, which was matter of great joy to us all and we bless God for such a mercy.'

THE EARLIEST SURVIVING KIRK SESSION MINUTES – DATED 7TH AUGUST 1651.

The minister enquired after the poor in the parish, requesting that the school be opened again. Of the baptisms in the village he heard a poignant tale: 'Until the ministers of Edinburgh came out of the Castle, which was about the later end of December, 1650, they carried the young children in to Edinburgh, some to Mr. John Adamson and some to Mr. William Arthure, who administered the sacrament of baptism.'

A small measure of stability now reached the parish, in that the children were back at their lessons, and the Session minutes record that the school was inspected by the heritors, the elders and the minister. Money was set aside by the Session for the poor in the parish, and even for some prisoners at Tynemouth Castle.

The elders' and minister's disciplining of the congregation was dispensed again with merciless regularity. Mild offenders were one parishioner who was brought to book for working in his waulk-mill on the Sabbath, and John Robinson of Bonaly who had to repent for drinking in the alehouse on the Sabbath with the English soldiers quartered on him. When the Session came to dealing with adultery, they had little compassion, often punishing with unyielding severity.

However, they did show some kindness when faced with the minister's serious illness. He became ill in 1658 and Mr John Charteris was called in to help Mr Livingstone, who had a 'sad weakness of the body'. A request was made to the Session to appoint a 'constant helper' for him, and after a preaching match among three ministers the Revd Robert Bennet was appointed in 1659 as assistant and successor in the Church of Hailes. The church, it seemed, then supported two ministers, for Mr Livingstone is recorded as being minister until he died in the parish in 1660. His parishioners must have forgiven him his flight from them in their time of need – they erected for him an imposing stone in the graveyard with a neatly lettered Latin inscription.

Mr Bennet then found himself in a parish of about 650 souls. Stretching from Corstorphine to Swanston, it still was fairly treeless and only small patches of land were drained and cultivated. The cot-houses would nestle mainly around the ford at Spylaw Street and Spylaw Bank Road, although there was a hamlet at Bonaly with waulk-mills, a skinnery, a distillery and a magnesia factory, and other small communities around the ferm-tounes.

A bridge had now been built across the ford. The men working on it were given two gallons and six pints of ale for their labours — and a porch was built on the church, the elders having complained 'how hard it was for them to stand without, collecting ye poores money in rainy weather having no shelter'.

The people, with their fragile dwellings and inadequate land drainage, were still at the mercy of the elements, and a terrible storm in 1659 caused untold damage to the crops and the mills.

John Nicoll, in his diary of the time, however, viewed the disaster wryly. It was, he wrote, a terrible judgment that followed the act of the Edinburgh Magistrates in putting an impost of a penny a pint on ale: 'When God frae the Heavens declared his anger by sending thunder and unheard of tempests and storms, and inundations of water whilk destroyit eleven mills ... with their dams, water gangs, timber graith and haill other works.'

The community could well have done without having to find wood to repair the mills. Timber was still so short that it had to be fetched from Queensferry to make communion tables. Even the Laird was conservation conscious. In his marriage contract with Barbara Ainslie of Dolphinton, Sir James Foulis gave her the 'manor house and dwelling place of Collington and yards for a dwelling house in her lifetime, providing she sufficiently maintains and upholds the said house in as good condition as they shall be at the time of Sir James' decease. And she shall not directly nor indirectly destroy any manner of grown trees or planting about the said house or yards or within any part of the bounds of Colinton for no pretext whatsoever'.

Vulnerable, often hungry, without any security in their homes, Mr Bennet's parishioners had plenty of problems to bring to him. He found soon, however, that he had problems of his own. In 1662 the Act of Uniformity was passed enforcing the practices of the Episcopal Church upon the churches of Scotland, and, sitting in the manse, he wrestled with his conscience about where he stood. The Session minutes state bleakly: 'No sessione by reason of all the Kirk Sessiones of the Church of Scotland was discharged by a publik declaration of the King's Majesty.'

Was Mr Bennet to be a king's man, a bishop's man? Was there to be another ousting in Colinton?

CHAPTER 6

The Trysting Place of all Colinton History

THE piece of land between Colinton churchyard gate and the Long Steps is barely 150 yards – indeed in early times most of it was a ford – yet for centuries it has been the trysting place of all Colinton history. Over here Prince Ethelred rode, planning his gift of a church for Hailes. Here came the monks from Dunfermline; here paced Vicar Richard in 1226, disputing with Thomas of Restalrig about the boundaries of the Hole Mill, and arguing with the Brothers of the Hospital of St Leonards in Edinburgh about the teinds of the Mill of Dreghorn; here walked the first Protestant minister of Colinton to take up his charge; here paused Cromwell's troops on their way to pillage Redhall and Colinton Castle; and here the Covenanters camped on their ill-fated journey to Rullion Green.

The boy Robert Louis Stevenson dreamed his dreams on this piece of land. The troops from Redford Barracks marched across it to attend service before going off to the trenches of the First World War. And on 3rd September 1939, the soldiers left the church early and crossed the bridge again, to ready themselves for the Second World War which they had been told had been declared while they sat in the Colinton Kirk pews.

It is a quiet leafy place now. On a summer's evening it seems to be peaceful and uneventful, but everywhere around there are the ghosts of a turbulent past.

Into the stormy times of 1662 walked the minister, the Revd Robert Bennet. The Act of Uniformity had just been passed and the Kirk Session disbanded. Bishops were back in power. Was he, the minister, to accept the rule of bishops which the Act now enforced, or was he to be whole-heartedly Presbyterian and resign his charge, as many of his colleagues were doing? How would the parishioners react if he stayed? Would they bundle him out, or let him be?

Apparently Mr Bennet was fortunate. The records show no immediate ousting, but Mr Bennet's troubles were only temporarily eased. In 1681 he was confronted with the Test Act. This was one of the most merciless pieces of legislation that Charles II forced on his subjects. The oath had to be taken by civil servants, members of parliament, bishops and ministers and teachers. Its purpose was uncompromising; it was to exclude from any of those occupations all Roman Catholics and Covenanters. Moreover, it asserted royal supremacy over the Church of Scotland. Many Presbyterians would not accept it and neither would many Episcopalians. Mr Bennet refused and found refuge in Ancrum, having been deprived of his parish by the government.

Whatever his views on royal supremacy and ecumenicism, Mr Bennet had shown little tolerance towards the shortcomings of his own flock in Colinton. With righteous zeal he and his elders persecuted and punished offenders, and the Session minutes read like one long indictment against the frailties of mankind.

Robert Duncan and William Balfour were hauled up before them and accused of the buying and selling of a Bible on the Sabbath. Robert confessed that he had taken a Bible from William, 'but would make no bargain with him upon that day'. The Session 'thought fitt they would be let goe with a rebuke'.

Working – or indeed doing anything on the Sabbath except going to church – was regarded as a serious sin. Visiting children or friends on the Lord's Day was condemned as a 'wicked custom'. The brewer at Graysmill was brought to book for brewing on the Lord's day – interestingly, she was a woman, and referred to as the Goodwife of Graysmill. Elders were appointed to snoop around the parish during service times on Sundays to try to catch any unfortunate miscreants.

To those who committed the sin of adultery the Session was merciless. The fact that their sovereign had an illegitimate son playing a prominent part in public affairs did not deter them. A sackcloth was specially made for the luckless George Gilchrist, who had to stand on a Sunday at the kirk door wearing this guilty garment, and afterwards go to the pillar inside the church, a place of public repentance, and be rebuked by the minister after the sermon. Four Sundays later, George was still sitting on the pillar in his sackcloth. His girlfriend, Bessie Vass, had a worse fate. At first she could not face the Session because of an illness; later she panicked: 'Bessie Vass, being called, did not compair. It was told she was fled out of the parish and none of the elders could learn where.' Where did poor Bessie find to go, and what became of her?

Superstition and fear of witchcraft were still rife in Mr Bennet's time. When a serving girl from the waulk-mill at Woodhall was found drowned in the river at Slateford, the neighbours 'especially those she served, did lay their hands upon her, but no blood did appear'. (It was believed that a murdered body bled if touched by the murderer.) The Session gave her a decent burial with money from the poors box – all she possessed were twenty shillings Scots, an old plaid and clothes 'which when seen were thought not worth twenty shillings Scots'.

THE 1630 MAP BY TIMOTHY PONT SHOWS THAT COLINTON WAS A SMALL SETTLEMENT BY THE RIVER, RINGED BY BARONIAL ESTATES.

Evil spirits had also to be kept at bay when there was a death in the parish. It was the beadle's job to walk down The Row – *ie* Spylaw Street – in front of funeral processions, ringing a handbell to frighten away the ghoulies from the burial. In 1678 the Session decided they needed a new handbell 'to ring before the dead', and this was purchased. New mortcloths for hiring to cover coffins had previously been bought, 'a larger and a lesser, for which was given near four hundred merks'.

Other practical matters had to be attended to. The communion tables were getting worse for wear, and it was decreed that the practice of lending them out for penny weddings should be stopped forthwith. The communion furnishings, which had suffered at the hands of Cromwell's men, had to be renewed. The Session decided that 'the treasurer buy linen for the communion tables and also bassines, there being non in the church before since the English, but always borrowed'. It was much regretted by the Session that they must take sums from the poors money to pay for the communion elements, 'but that they see no help for it without a visitation of the kirk. Some of the heritors are willing to give something gratis for the effect, but they will not be bound for it nor acknowledge it a just debt'. There were to be many more battles with the heritors concerning their obligations to the financing of church needs.

The event for which Mr Bennet's ministry in Colinton will most be remembered for, however, had nothing to do with the refurbishing of the church, or even with his refusal to take the Test. It was the battle of Rullion Green.

On 27th November 1666, a cold blustery day, there straggled on to the bridge by the kirk a weary band of peasant troops, who had begun their revolt in the south-west of Scotland. In that area the repression against the Covenanters by government troops under Sir James Turner had been particularly severe. It was not surprising, therefore, that when Turner was captured in Dumfries by some local people, the torch was lit for open rebellion against the fines for non-attendance at church and the quenching of freedom to worship, Covenanter-fashion, at the private conventicles. Putting a heavy guard by the side of their much-prized prisoner, they set their faces north, taking Turner with them.

At Lanark the rebels managed to muster a sizable army and, knowing that it was not yet the time to face their main opponent, General Tam Dalziel of the Binns, they evaded him and approached Edinburgh via Bathgate, expecting that the men of Linlithgowshire were ready to join them. At Colinton Bridge, exhausted and hungry after their days on the march, they learned the worst. There was no large column of men flocking to their standard, the city of Edinburgh was well defended against them and they could not expect help from even their own party there. Indeed, a message had been sent to them, carried by a woman, telling them that the Cowgate Port was secured and assuring them that they would not succeed since they had not cut Sir James Turner's throat. In the blinding snow conditions, however, the woman lost her way and the message never reached them.

A good proportion of the rebels were mere boys, and all were ill-equipped for such a venture. The wild weather also seemed to be against their cause. As a consequence, large numbers slipped away back home, and by the decisive date of 27th November the army was reduced to barely nine hundred.

Turner, in his memoirs, described clearly where they camped: 'The place where they quartered, by reason of a church and churchyard, a stone bridge, the water, because of the great raines, unfoordable, was defencible enough against infalls.'

They camped in the valley near the church. He himself fared better. In fact he seems to have been remarkably well treated by his captors in the circumstances, because he and his guards were put up in the 'best inne', although he admitted he feared that his throat would be cut before the morning.

Wallace and most of his officers gave me a visite. He told me that he was more troubled for me than for himselfe; for he found it would be convenient for him to stay in the field most of that night, which he thought would not be fit for me to doe, and therefor askd me, if I wold not stay in my lodgeing with my guards. Bot I apprehending my guard might have order rather to dispatch me, then suffer me to be taken from them, told him, I wold rather choose to goe to the field with him. While we were speaking thus, the noyce of tuo pistolls gave ane alarm; Wallace presentlie left me, bot left order with my guard to keepe me in my lodgeing till his further direction.

At about two or three o'clock in the morning there was a scuffle between the rebels and some of the government forces, but in the morning the leaders marched their dispirited troops up the Loan, across the Braid Burn, past Dreghorn and Swanston, and then they turned south to Biggar. Here on 28th November they camped at Rullion Green and met their fate at the hands of Dalziel and the Royalists, who had come round the shoulder of the hill from Currie. At least 52 Covenanters were killed and 150 were taken prisoner. Some of these were transported to slavery in the sugar plantations of Barbados, but thirty were executed for refusing to take the oath of allegiance.

A monument on the windswept hill of Rullion Green now

THE COVENANTERS' MONUMENT, REDFORD ROAD, ERECTED BY MR R A MACFIE OF DREGHORN IN 1884.

marks the spot where the battle was fought – one of the saddest events in Scottish history – but there is not one single contemporary reference to it in the Colinton Kirk Session Records, though the poignant story unfolded itself on the kirk's very doorstep.

There was more religious violence to come. After the murder of the Episcopal Church's Archbishop Sharp by fanatical Covenanters, and the consequent disarray in both political and religious spheres, elders everywhere awaited anxiously the outcome of the confrontation in 1679 between the Covenanters and the Royalists at Bothwell Bridge. When news of the Convenanters' total defeat reached the Colinton Session, they recorded: 'Because the tymes were troublesome for it was at ye tyme of Bothwell Bridge, the sessione desyred ye tresaurer to secure the poors money.' And in August it was written: 'The communion was delayed this year by reasone of the troublesome tyme, the countrie being in confussione which was occasioned by the fight at Bothwell Bridge.'

Times seem to have been a little easier the following year, for the Session saw fit to buy two handsome silver Communion cups, engraved not only with suitable biblical quotations, but with the firm statement: 'This Cup belongs to the Kirk sessione of Collingtoune.' It is to be hoped that there were not too many hungry parishioners around at the time, for the cups were bought with the 'poors money'. The next year they did some repairs to the church and in due course also to the schoolmaster's house. Neither the kirk nor the manse can have been in a very sound state, because the heritors were asked again in 1684 and 1695 to pay up for further repairs, and to build a barn for the minister close by the Hole Mill, a request they were very unwilling to comply with.

Mr Bennet's last year in the parish was a troubled one, but his difficulties, however, were minimal compared with those of some of his parishioners. Take the poignant case of poor Helen Girdwood, which is recorded with rare lack of condemnation, even with compassion, in the Session Records of 8th February 1680:

A sad accident fell out in this parish; one Helen Girdwood a servant in Caldhame did bring furth a child in ye said towne, att ye back of ye dyks. Nae body with her, in a cold day, albeit she has a sister

> *living in the same towne, and accidentaly a midwyfe in ye towne at ye very tyme who was comed to see a woman lying in chyldbed there. After she had brought forth the child she laid it in the tilled land, and covered it in the red ground, and so came unto the house and lay down upon a bed and said that she had a vehement colleck.*
>
> *Within a little space after, the swine about the house finding the smell of the child, followed the scent of the child, and were seen presently by a herd lade, snuffing and grinkling about the child, and had put the red ground off it; the child was taken up and brought in, and laid beforr her bedsyd upon a chest; she had nothing to say for herself, but that the child was borne dead, and that when she went out to the back of the dyke, she had not a purpose to bear her child; she said the child was to one William Pennie, miller in the new mylne of Redhall, a man which hath a wife, and three children: the man was brought before her, and confessed that he was the father of the child. The woman within a few days after was sent to the Tolbooth of Edinburgh, where she yet remains; as for the man, his satisfying of the church is delayed until the woman receive her sentence.*

The Session were still paying attention to the superstitions of the time: 'There was one thing very observable in that business that when the mother laid her hand upon the child's nose there came a little blood from its nose which was seen by many present ....'

For poor Helen there remained little hope. This appalling postscript was written on the 15th August of the same year:

> *The woman Helen Girdwood, who murdered her child as is said before, was executed at the Grassmarket in Edinburgh. William Pennie, father of the child, after he had appeared befor the Presbyterie in sackcloth, did stand at ye church door here in sackcloth, and sat upon the pillar in sackcloth, half a year, professing a great deal of grief and sorrow.*

He was eventually absolved 'att ye Presbyteries' desire'.

When the Revd Thomas Murray took over the parish from Mr Bennet in 1682, he came to a community of fewer than four hundred souls. He found that the stretch of the Water of Leith which ran through the parish worked its passage not only by providing water for the animals, the bleaching and the household needs, but by turning the wheels of half a dozen mills. (It must have been extremely noisy for him in the manse, with the Hole Mill clanking away behind his garden – no wonder he complained to the Session when he did not even get peace on the Sabbath because of the mill.) As he went out to visit his flock, passing the dominie's house at his gate, he would hear the children chanting away at their lessons, and further up the hill there were the age-old sounds of the blacksmith, the carpenter and the handloom weaver.

In the heritors' houses, however, there were big changes. The lairds' families had come to appreciate not only beautiful surroundings, but a far more varied diet than had been available in the past. They began to create great gardens.

At Colinton Castle the holly hedges, which had been planted recently, were growing well. Designed as boundaries for two shrubbery gardens and the kitchen garden, they had a pleasant broad grass walk in between them. Gardeners were consulted and began to have status in the community. The Colinton gardener even wrote a treatise on his subject, which was a century later to be considered 'a very sensible performance' by the writer Henry Mackenzie when he read it.

The local lairds still took a prominent part in the country's affairs, and one of the topics discussed most vehemently at that time was the proposed Union of the Parliaments of England and Scotland, negotiations for which had been opened in 1670. If Mr Murray went up the road to Redford House to see Lord Redford, he would have known exactly where his host stood on the issue. Lord Redford, who was on the bench beside his father, Lord Colinton, was firmly a Home Rule man, opposing the suggested union at every stage of the debate.

All round the parish, too, Mr Murray would hear grumblings about the hated Hearth Tax, brought into force in 1683. There were 277 taxable hearths in Colinton Parish and, interestingly, in the original document the parish was spelt as it is now spelt, whereas there were still many variations in other sources.

Mr Murray did not tarry long at Colinton – perhaps the noise

REDFORD HOUSE – SCENE OF MANY ARGUMENTS ABOUT THE PROPOSED UNION OF PARLIAMENTS OF ENGLAND AND SCOTLAND. LORD REDFORD OPPOSED IT.

of the Hole Mill behind the manse was too much for him. In any event he demitted the charge and went to Kinloch in 1685. It was 1686 before the vacancy committee found the Revd Samuel Nimmo to succeed him – a strange choice, for he had strong Episcopal principles which brought to the Session innumerable difficulties. Even the Session Clerk seems to have been defeated by the complexities of the situation, for there is a gap in the records from 24th February 1689 to 21st May 1694.

Mr Nimmo's time, therefore, was singularly unrecorded, yet it was tempestuous. In 1691 he became another minister at Colinton to pack his bags in a hurry; he was deprived by the General Assembly for refusing to recognise the authority of the Presbytery as it was then established, or to acknowledge the Revolution Settlement which deposed King James VII and put William and Mary on the throne.

Stubbornly he had continued to pray publicly for King James, the 'profest Papist'. It was all very confusing for the Colinton people. There was bound to be trouble. Yet, when the case came before the Privy Council, they did not pronounce Mr Nimmo guilty of a crime. The men of Argyll's Regiment, however, were not so lenient. On 27th April 1689, Samuel Nimmo and his family were alarmed by forty armed men invading the house, with 'wicked and bloodie designe' against the minister. Mr Nimmo's own words in his Petition to the Estates describe the event graphically:

And makeing strick search for, and having missed the petitioner [himself], they caused the Reader and the Beddell tear his gowne. And then most sacralegiouslie took away the vessels of the Sanctuarie. And all this allanarlie [solely] *because he is one of the regular Clergie, who was called to serve the Cure ther by consent of the haill people. And alleadgeing they hade ane order, they made peremptor warneing for him and his famillie to flitt and remove them within six dayes and that under the highest perrill.*

Discretion seemed suddenly to be the better part of valour, for Mr Nimmo finally agreed to pray for William and Mary, and the Committee of the Estates within a week requested the heritors to protect their minister 'in the exercise of his ministry and in the possession of his house'.

This, though, was only a temporary abatement of the harrying – within a few months Episcopacy was formally abolished and the Established Church became Presbyterian. Now the elders had a new duty – to hunt down not only Papists, but any Episcopalians in the parish. Mr William Irvine, an Episcopal minister sheltering with the Foulis family at Colinton Castle, was investigated, but 'was not touched because he did not act as a chaplain in Collingtown's familie'. The General Assembly was not, however, lenient to practising Episcopalian ministers and the die was cast for Mr Nimmo who found he could not adopt Presbyterian ways. He had to go.

He seems to have been left in peace, however, for he lived until the good age of 74 years.

Meanwhile the Session, after the incident with Argyll's soldiers, deemed it prudent to hide the 'Kirk goods'. Adam Thomson, a tenant in Bonaly, undertook to hide the Register Book, the Communion cups and Kirk Bible until less troublesome times.

During the vacancy, news of national events filtered into the taverns – there had been a massacre at Glencoe; there was talk of establishing a Scottish trading station at Darien in Central

America; and the government were bringing in a Poll Tax – as if the Hearth Tax had not been bad enough. Colinton itself was altering; the lairds were enclosing their fields and, backed by legislature, were disentangling the run-rig system. The new ways may have made for better farming but did not always improve the lot of individual tenants. The Commonty of the Pentlands, where everyone had been able to graze their animals, was to be officially divided among the owners – and many a dispute there was to be over that. The Winter Herding Act, which had been passed a few years earlier, caused everyone much more work. It pronounced that 'heretors, liferenters, tenents and cotters ... herd their horses, sheep, swyne and goats the wholl year as weel in winter as in summer and in night tyme shall causc keep the same in houses, folds or inclosures'. Parliament saw the necessity of protecting the remaining unfenced crops and young trees.

It was a time of change for the new minister, too. It had now been decided by the General Assembly that a minister should be called under the true Presbyterian system, and so a law dating from Cromwell's rule was renewed, giving the responsibility of choosing a minister back to the congregation – or at least to some of them. When the Revd James Thomson came to Colinton in 1694, therefore, he was appointed by the heritors, the elders and the lairds. The Session thought it was now safe to get the 'Kirk goods' out of hiding at Bonaly.

The parish would seem to have earned a little stability, but it was not to be so. Mr Thomson stayed barely more than a year, then left for Elgin. Next in the manse was Mr Thomas Paterson in 1697, but he also did not remain long, and departed for St Cuthbert's, Edinburgh, in 1699. The Session, no doubt weary of coping with vacancies, attended the Presbytery and opposed the proposed removal, but they failed in their attempt. With the next minister, the Revd Walter Allan, they were, however, more fortunate. He had been chaplain to Sir John Foulis at Woodhall and clearly liked Colinton. He stayed for 32 years, married twice, filled the manse with five children and died still minister of the parish. At Mr Allan's induction Sir John saw to it that there was a great dinner for his protégé, with lots of ale, brandy, beef, mutton, rabbits, fowls, bread, twelve bottles of claret and four bottles of sack. The tobacco alone at the meal cost two shillings.

This feasting seems inappropriate, for by now the parish, like the rest of Scotland, was suffering the Seven Ill Years, 1697–1704, when unprecedented blight and famine hit the country. Fletcher of Saltoun left this contemporary account: 'two hundred thousand vagrants begging from door to door, half of these belonging to the wild, brutalised savage race of nomads, the other half families whom poverty and famine had driven to want, while thousands of our people are at this day dying for want of food.' It was said that in many parishes a third of the inhabitants died. Some villages simply went into ruin and disappeared.

Yet, through all these appalling times, the church was obliged to remember its Christian duty elsewhere. The parish was required to collect money for fellow Protestants to found a church at Konisberg in Prussia, and to help redeem nine slaves and captives in Barbary. At home they had to provide for the education of all the parish children, for the 1696 Education Act established that there had to be a school in every parish in Scotland.

The Session and the heritors, overwhelmed by the adversities of the times, when they met to choose their new minister in 1700 deemed an all-purpose fast was called for. The fact that so many of the parishioners around them were involuntarily fasting did not seem to deter them. The purposes of the fast were spelled out:

> *For a good seedtime, and because there was pinching dearth, great sickness, and mortality, the rebukes of God in the nation in disappointing overall undertakings to advance in the cross providences that the African and Indian Companys Colonie in Africa has met weith, the heart plagues of security, and impenitency, the fearsome backslidings, and persecutions of the late times, notwithstanding of solemn covenants and engadgments, atheisticall principalls so much vented and spread among us, the immoralities of uncleanness of all sorts, the great slighting of the Gospell, the stupendious burning of a piece of Edinburgh, the deplorable state of the reformed churches in France, and for our King's Majesties.*

Young Mr Allan had his work cut out for him when he came down the road from Woodhall to take up residence in the manse.

CHAPTER 7

The Coming of the Nouveaux Riches

THE beginning of the eighteenth century not only brought changes in farming methods to Colinton, it brought a new kind of laird. Land began to be sold by some of the long established gentry, impoverished by political misfortunes or bad luck. (Baberton changed hands as a result of the turn of a card.) The new owners were often burgesses and successful businessmen, who saw as desirable the possession of a country house. Retaining their cramped town houses up the closes of the High Street for the winter months, these merchants, millers and coachbuilders settled their families into the green spaces of Colinton in the summer. Equipping themselves with coaches and riding horses, they travelled back and forth to Edinburgh to see to their businesses. The age of commuting had begun.

JAMES GILLESPIE

The most famous of those new country gentlemen was to be James Gillespie who in 1759 took over the feu of Spylaw mill and house, 'with the privilege of a cart road from Colinton to the mill and also of a foot road from the north end of Colinton Bridge to the mill'. For this he paid £18.1s.6d and an annual feu duty of £1.4s.6d – sums he raised with no difficulty from his profitable business of milling snuff. While he personally supervised the work in the mill, which was immediately behind his house at Spylaw Park, his brother was in charge of the shop in Edinburgh. They made enough money at Spylaw for bachelor James to confound any hopeful inheritors by bequeathing his estate at

Colinton, plus £12,000 Scots to the Company of Merchants to be used for the care of old men and women. The present-day pantiled houses in The Row were funded as alms houses out of this endowment trust and the Merchant Company of Edinburgh still has feudal superiority over much land in Colinton, thanks to James Gillespie.

> *Wha wad hae thocht it,*
> *that noses had bocht it ...*

was a facetious contemporary suggestion for a motto to be painted on the side of the carriage that took James Gillespie in and out of town.

Gillespie's handsome mausoleum still stands in the graveyard of Colinton Kirk. Five years before his death, he paid £5.5s to the poor of the parish for the privilege of being allowed by the Kirk Session to enclose a piece of the graveyard 'to erect thereon a monument or tomb for a burying place for his family'. Six hundred years on from the days of Prince Ethelred, the wealthy in Colinton still considered it important to have a grand resting-place.

Among them was the Foulis family who still lived at Colinton Castle, though their fortunes never recovered from their uncompromising stand against Cromwell in 1650, and the plundering and destruction of their property that followed. Over the years parcels of the Foulis lands had to be sold off, often to the *nouveaux riches* coming out from town; yet the family, as long-established landowners and heritors of the post-Reformation church, managed to cling on to their aristocratic position in the community. The villagers of Colinton, when they passed Lord Colinton on Spylaw Street, still pulled a forelock to him, or bobbed a curtsey.

Another branch of the Foulis family, on the other hand, was flourishing. Sir James Foulis' cousin, Sir John Foulis of Ravelston, bought the estate of Woodhall, together with the paper-mills of Spylaw and some waulk-mills, and, moving over to Colinton, he threw himself vigorously into his duties as a landowner and kirk heritor.

He loved Woodhall, his new house, and spent a lot of money enlarging and improving it.

I have agreed with Laurie Henderson for painting the roume of the hall whyte japand pannels, black borders, with pictures of flowers, men, etc. and gilded, the cornish marble chimney marble and surbase marble, the picture frames japand, with flowers of all sorts, etc. for 10 pounds sterl., and what I pleased to give more, he sought 11 pounds.

And was it Sir John who purloined two seventeenth century Y-tracery windows which were perhaps lying about after the demolition of the Medieval Colinton Kirk, and incorporated them into the wall of his dovecote? Was it he who built into the house at the left of the front door a piece of ancient graveyard sculpture which decorates, in a rather awesome way, that blank wall?

While embellishing his new country house at Woodhall, Sir John kept on his town house at Foster's Wynd off the High Street, and now embarked upon the life typical of many of the successful men in the neighbourhood, going in and out of town by coach for business purposes, for entertainment and for sport. He was an extremely practical man, and he left as a priceless legacy his Account Book of 1671–1707, whose detailed entries paint a vivid picture of what life was like for a country gentleman in Colinton at that time.

At Woodhall the daily diet was rich and varied. They ate mutton, beef, pigeons from the dovecote and game, but in addition larks (ordered two dozen at a time), oysters, and Solan geese – gannets, brought from the Bass Rock. Also on the table were pomegranates, Spanish nuts, figs, lemons and oranges, with coffee and hot chocolate. Indeed Sir John itemises so frequently the price of a 'chopin of wine' or 'ale and brandy', that he clearly had a good cellar too.

In the gardens they grew leeks, onions, beetroot, cauliflower, spinach, sugar peas, Indian cress, Silesia lettuce, radishes and celery. From George Keir, the gardener at Colinton Castle, they got

Sir John Foulis' Woodhall House did not have baronial castellations, hoodmoulds over the windows or the Central Tower. Nevertheless he embellished it greatly.

grafts from plum trees and pear trees, and '3 setts of stript hollie'. There was more planting with young firs, beeches, oaks, grafts of apricots from Heriot's workyards, and clover seed which was sewn in the north pathway of the west orchard.

Prices were also obtained for cherry trees, raspberry canes, strawberry plants, parsnips, turnips, artichokes and potatoes, which were a new vegetable in Scotland. Sir John liked flowers as well. He had David Wilson, his gardener, plant tulips, white lilies, pinks, anemones and lavender, much of which was brought over from Corstorphine. The orchard and gardens of Woodhall were enclosed by dykes and thorn hedges and the animals grazed on Sir John's portion of the Commonty of the Pentlands.

The hunt was a way of life of the gentlemen of the neighbourhood, as was hawking and fishing. Other entertainment was playing lant, a card game at which Sir John frequently lost money, attending the races at Leith and going to the theatre there. (One of the plays he saw was 'Macbeth', and on another occasion he took his grandson to see an elephant, and, perhaps to its surprise, they gave it bread and ale.)

Sir John was a keen golfer and went to the links at Leith for his game. The purchase of golf balls features in the accounts, and six shillings for a golf club for his son Archie in 1672, who was then only nine years old. Later his young grandsons were also given golf clubs. Occasionally Sir John curled, and he frequently enjoyed a game of bowls at Pratt's Green in the Potter Row, sometimes with 'young Dreghorne'.

There had to be ready cash for tipping Lord Colinton's coachman, for getting the laundry bleached by the 'bleicher wife at Bonaley', for Mr Strachan in the Canongate for clock repairs, and for the packman for mousetraps. Vermin at Woodhall seem to have been quite a problem – there is an entry 'to the barbour lad for barbarising and dressing my wig ye ratts did eat'.

As a heritor Sir John contributed to the 'cart custom' which brought 100 slates out to Colinton Kirk, but another transaction at the kirk in 1702 sounds strictly economical:

March 2 ... wife has given 3 ells and 1/2 fyne black cloath that covered the seat in the kirk to be her sone roberts cloathes.

Frequently figuring in the Accounts are sums for 'bread and ale with Colintounes familie and us at ye kirk'. Did they have a picnic at the church between the lengthy services? Sometimes there was also brandy in the basket.

The blacksmith, Wattie Waddie at Torphin, did much work for Sir John, seeing to the Shetland pony, which perhaps was provided for the grandchildren at Woodhall to ride, and of course shoeing the horses regularly. He even bled them, according to medical practice. Sir John, appreciative of his blacksmith's efforts, gave him a gift of money at his wedding – indeed contributions to local penny weddings and the fiddlers were made several times.

Sir John's family tomb was at Greyfriars Church near his town house, but as a heritor and landowner at Colinton he also maintained an 'Ile' at the local church.

1702, May 14: To robt johstoun, belman at colingtoune, to take care of ye Ile.

In 1703 Jon Miller, the slater, was paid for work on the Ile at the Kirk of Colinton, and in 1705 Joseph Beitch was paid for painting the door of Colinton Kirk black and for 'painting black the Ile'.

Sir John was a man who liked to follow the customs of the times. When his third wife died, he gave money to several churches to remember her in prayer, he put a special collection in at the kirk door 'ye Sunday after my dear wife was removed', and he paid for funeral drummers, pipers and beadles. He had a new black handle put on his black sword, mourning clothes, and of course had an expensive mortcloth made for her coffin.

Only a year later his daughter-in-law and his infant grandson died at Woodhall and Sir John had to get out his mourning clothes again. His daughter, Jean, was given money to 'buy a pair of whyt gloves for the corps', and Mrs Aitkine was paid for making the 'dead cloathes' for William's wife and baby son.

In spite of the severe ways thieves were dealt with, there seems to have been trouble in Colinton with burglars, for Sir John more than once had new locks and keys made. He apparently felt he could not leave unlocked the milk-house, the coal house, the stable and the washing house.

Agricultural improvements also went ahead at Woodhall. Land was taken in from the moor, and it was harrowed and planted with oats and hemp seed. More land was enclosed with dykes and thorns, and trees planted on the 'intake'. To this day there can be seen remnants of hedgerow pattern which may well belong to Sir John's time. They run down the west side of Bonaly Road, both sides of Fernielaw Avenue, the south side of West Carnethy Avenue and along the back of the southern Munro Drive gardens. There are also still vestiges of enclosure at Woodhall.

In 1704 there were celebrations down at the manse, because the minister's wife had given birth to a son and the beadle was rewarded for bringing the news to Woodhall. His tip was also for 'taking care of the Ile', but more drastic measures were needed than the beadle could handle. Wattie Waddie, the blacksmith, had to be employed to fix three 'kneed strips to the stoups' – metal bands to strengthen the pillars – of the seat and loft in the kirk. Irreparable structural damage was to be diagnosed in the church building in 1771 – it seems that the trouble had already begun.

In May 1707 the entries cease abruptly, but not before it is recorded that Sir John had visits from the doctor for bloodletting, payment was made for 'coloured knittings' for tying up the documents of Woodhall by the lawyer, and arrangements were made about his will for his fourth wife. On his last birthday in February he had a chopin of wine, and in March, Mr Walter Allan, his former chaplain and now the minister, came for dinner. Sir John was still busy about the estate, paying Robert Wilson for shooting hoodie crows, and David and James Zets for taking down the magpie's nest. A distressed stranger was given some money in charity, and, finally, John Simsone in Bonaly paid his 1706 rent. In this, Sir John's last recorded entry before the tomb at Greyfriars claimed him, he noted that this rent-money was given to his wife.

If John Simsone of Bonaly ever heard of this gift, he would have taken little comfort from it. The Lady of Woodhall, he would think, was not in need of the obligatory rent which he had raised with such difficulty. When he set off for Woodhall from the small settlement of cot-houses at Bonaly, which were clustered round the modest farmhouse destined to be extended and castellated in the next century into Lord Cockburn's country seat, his mind would be burdened with worries about the haymaking, the coming harvest and the family's health.

Trudging by the Bonaly cottages of Adam Tomsone, John Broune and old Robert Finlay, then past the homes of young Robert Finlay and Marion Wilson at Fernielaw, and finally west at the foot of the hill over the land newly taken in from the moor for the Woodhall Estate by James David and his men, he would see little evidence of prosperity among the labouring people. Here he was, having to find £16.3s.4d Scots of rent-money for old Sir John Foulis who had never lacked a shilling for his snuff, gaming and fancy clothes, when the countryside and the people around him were still reeling from the effects of the Seven Hungry Years – or, as the Jacobites came to call them, 'King William's Years'.

Apart from the odd gift to charity, Sir John's Account Book gives no reflection of the devastation taking place around him in Scotland. When he was convivially losing money at cards or golf, or enthusiastically ordering fine panel paintings of flowers for his hall at Woodhall, his neighbours in the Dell and up at Bonaly were dying of disease and malnutrition. When he was buying expensive chamois leather gloves for himself, and ordering a silk nightgown and matching slippers for his fourth wedding, John at Bonaly was looking in anguish at the crops blighted by early frosts and summers of continual haar, and at the sheep on the Pentlands suffering from lack of grazing.

There is recorded the finding of a mass grave in the eighteenth century on the land now known as Dovecote Park. Could it be that this hasty burial of so many people at once dates from the time of the Seven Hungry Years in Colinton, when no church sexton could cope with the demands made upon him?

In the taverns in the village at this time, however, the talk was not only of the hard times, but of an Act of Union of the Parliaments of England and Scotland. What was for the best? Over at Redford House, Lord Redford, they knew, was fiercely against it. The eldest son of Sir James Foulis of Colinton, he was a High Court Judge and a Privy Councillor. He had not welcomed the succession of William and Mary a few years earlier, and although he signed the Act declaring that the Scottish Convention was, in fact, a lawful meeting of the Estates, he would not go so far as to sign a letter of congratulation to King William.

When the Union debate was under way in earnest, tales of the violence and vehemence that greeted the nation's representatives as they arrived in the High Street to seal the fate of Scotland must have reached Colinton. Anti-English pamphlets were pushed from hand to hand in the taverns and coffee-houses.

Elsewhere in the country there were also stormy scenes of opposition, and slogans against the Hanoverians, whose succession was to be part of the Union bargain, were shouted around the streets. Only after the Act of Security of the Church of Scotland was passed and incorporated into the Act of Union, did any undecided Presbyterians agree to the Union, but Lord Redford, whose family had Episcopalian leanings, never wavered in his opposition. At some point over the centuries an owner of Redford House embellished it with an ornamental stone carving of a rose on one gable-end and a thistle on the other. Lord Redford has had the last laugh, for the rose on the east gable has fallen off and disappeared into the mists of time, but the thistle to this day proudly stands on the western gable.

It was only eleven days after the Act of Union had received Royal assent when John Simsone of Bonaly plodded down the hill to Woodhall to hand over his yearly rent for the last time to Sir John Foulis, yet the political turmoil which had seethed around him so recently was to have little effect on his livelihood. His £16.3.4d was still to go to the Lady of Woodhall, for her to buy new shoes and gloves, wall-hangings for her fine home and exotic oranges for her table. When John returned home there might be nettle soup, some bannocks and, if he was lucky, a pigeon that had been handed to him by William Denhame at the Mains of Woodhall to celebrate the achievement of managing to hand over the rent.

From the church John got some solace, however. At last the minister, Mr Allan, had restored communion – they had not celebrated it for fourteen years because of the preceding tumultuous times. By now there was great difficulty in getting a full complement of elders. Perhaps not everyone relished the role of spying upon, and sitting in judgment on his neighbours. A recruiting drive was embarked upon by the Session, but without much success.

They were looking for men who 'have familie worship by

prayer reading and singing, because it is a duty agreeable to the word of God and recommended by the General Assembly'. Even a personal approach by the minister to some of the tenant farmers did not increase the numbers, and only one of the heritors, Mr David Pitcairn of Dreghorn, was an elder. Either privately or publicly, the lairds still cherished a liking for Episcopacy.

However, the work of the Session still went on. They reported with satisfaction that 'there are no Papists residing in our Parish'. They gave help to a woman who had given birth to quads, and also to seamen who had come home from 'two years creuell and tyranicall slaverie' in Turkey.

Then there was the poignant case of little Jine of Redford, 'a female child, supposed to be about eight weeks old', who was found in the garden of Redford House. An emergency meeting of the Session decided that a nurse must be provided immediately for the little foundling, and paid 16s.3d a quarter. They realised, of course, that the matter would not rest there, for if they could not find the baby's mother they would be responsible for bringing her up until she was old enough to work. So the foundling was 'advertised in the public Prints', and 4s.6d was paid out for 'prosecuting a person suspected to be the foundling's mother before the Justices of the Peace'.

Nothing came of all this expenditure, for the payments go on for Jine's maintenance, and soon the items of clothing begin. There was 'a gown' when she was 18 months old, costing 4d, made for her by the local tailor James Anderson who made clothes for other poor children and mended the mortcloths. Then there were shoes when little Jine was two and a half years old – two pairs a year – and '4 sarks for Jine Redford the Foundling'. It was customary then to give an abandoned child the name of the place where he or she was found, but perhaps to abolish any stigma that may have been attached to Jine for this, the Session began, when she was nine years old, to refer to her as Jine Foord.

When Jine had smallpox, the Session paid for her medicines; and when she was 10 years old her education was well underway, for she was provided with paper, pen and ink. But the final payment came in the Session Account Book when Jine was 11 years 3 months old – a nest-egg of £2.17s.8$^{1}/_{2}$d. By now the Session had decided that Jine could look after herself. What became of her? Did Jine, aged 11, find work all by herself, spinning and weaving? Did someone in the parish have mercy and take her in?

By the early eighteenth century there were nearly 800 'examinable persons' in Colinton Church – people eligible for Communion – which meant that so many people flocked down to the Dell on Communion Sunday that they had to stand outside and Mr Allan preached to them from a Punch-and-Judy type of structure known as a 'tent'. His stipend was raised, although part of it was still paid in kind. There was, nevertheless, little money to spare, and in 1712 the trees in the minister's yard were felled to raise cash to repair the church and churchyard dykes. The heritors had to find the balance. But much worse was to come for them.

Who were the heritors? In essence, they were the landlords of a parish, or their representatives, who had inherited the role of maintaining the fledgling Church of Scotland, the largest slice of the revenues of the Roman Catholic Church at the Reformation having been appropriated by the Crown and those who had acquired its land. In Colinton, therefore, the heritors were the landlords of Hailes, Colinton Castle, Comiston, Mortonhall, Colinton Mains, Dreghorn, Spylaw, Woodhall, Redford and Craiglockhart. They found themselves responsible for providing and maintaining 'the requisites of religious ministration within the Parish'. The church was 'vested in trust with the heritors for the use of parishioners in public worship'.

In practice this meant that they had to keep the roof on the parish school and find a suitable schoolmaster, they had to look after the upkeep of the church, the churchyard and the manse, which by Church statute had to include a stable, barn, byre, pig-sty, garden wall, water supply and glebe. They also had to contribute to poor relief in the parish. All this was quite a commitment: not surprisingly the church sometimes had difficulty

GRAYSMILL FARM, WHERE PRINCE CHARLES EDWARD STEWART STAYED BEFORE MAKING HIS ENTRANCE TO HOLYROOD IN 1745, WAS A TYPICAL 18TH CENTURY COLINTON FARM.

getting enough money out of the heritors to keep things going.

There were some rewards. The heritors could build handsome pews and lofts within the church for themselves, their guests and their tenants, the size of which was determined by the valued rent of each heritor's property. Indeed, these lofts became so elaborate that their sheer weight contributed greatly to the rapid deterioration of the fabric of the church. They must have surely regretted their grandiose ideas when the church began to fall down and they found that they were responsible for building a new one.

The crisis over the safety of the building was becoming apparent during the ministry of the Revd Walter Allan, but it had not come to a head before his death in 1732. (The stone his 'sorrowfull Relict Isobell Brown' had put over his grave in the churchyard still stands. She had inscribed on it that he had 'diligently and faithfully discharged the dutys of that sacred office in this paroch for the space of 32 years'. He was only 54 years when he died.)

His successor, the Revd George Gibson, however, had other things on his mind than the fabric of the church or the manse.

When he took office in 1733, he found himself coping with the problems raised by the First Secession, a break-away movement from the Established Church, which was caused mainly by the emotive issue of patronage. This was the question of whether the patron of a church, whose appointment usually went hand-in-hand with a land deal or a royal reward, had the right to foist his personal choice of minister on to a congregation, or whether the congregation could choose its own minister.

George Gibson did not join the Seceders, and was therefore at the manse when an extraordinary event took place over at Graysmill. In 1745 the Young Pretender, Prince Charles Edward Stewart, arrived on his way to Holyrood, and bivouacked with his troops on David Wright's field of nearly-ripe pease.

Prince Charles Edward's presence was by no means welcomed by everyone. Poor David, for instance, had a job getting compensation for his ruined crop. Firstly he approached the Prince himself, who was staying at the farmhouse, but he had little faith in a promissory note offered to him in the name of 'Prince Regent'. An amused Prince Charles then suggested that the name of the Duke of Perth might be more acceptable as a credit-worthy guarantor and David was satisfied – but nothing could immediately replace his damaged crops.

Others were also disenchanted with the young Prince and his followers. A contemporary account by the Laird of Woodhouselee, near Roslin, described the passing of the Young Pretender's cavalcade 'and all the Highland wifes' as follows:

> ... *and on they came, with their bagpipes and plaids, rusty rapiers, matchlocks and firelocks, and tag rag and bob tail was there.*
>
> *I crossed their road after they had past Morton and come up with ane honest farmer in Collington Mains, whose horses and carriages they had pressed. He told me they had plundered and broke all his furniture, they had robbed 6 silver spoons. I took off by the by-road to Brade and went down to Canaan Muir, and at a distance had a politer sight. This was the pretended Prince, his retinue and guards.*

It has to be said that this writer may have been somewhat

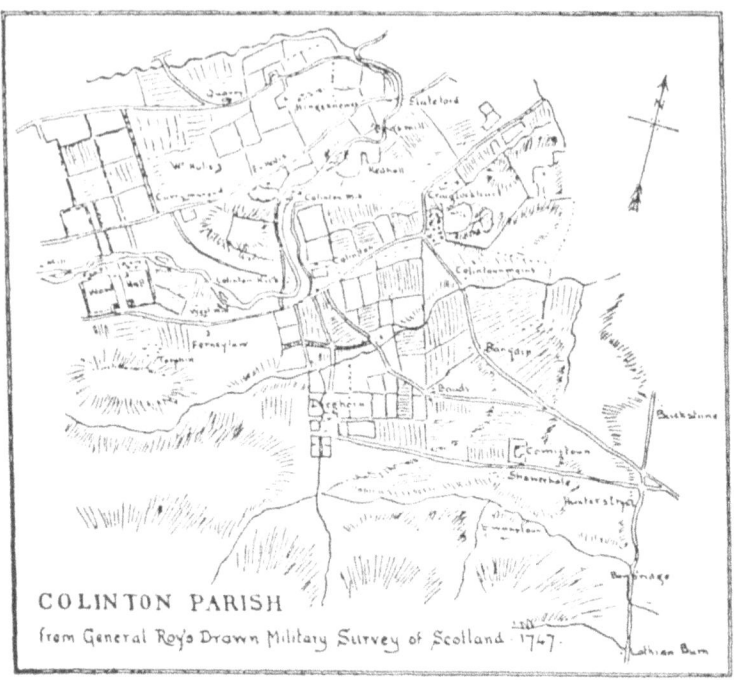

COLINTON PARISH
from General Roy's Drawn Military Survey of Scotland 1747.

biased in his account. He was a committed Whig, and a staunch Presbyterian: 'Who that has a drop of British blood in his wame can befriend a Popish Prince with a manifesto dated at Rome?' he asked.

After the Battle of Prestonpans, the Woodhouselee laird again wrote of the events around him. At Buckstone he met a group of countrymen from Swanston, who had three Highland captives. 'They were using them not tenderly, but the gang have irritated the country by their pilfering and oppression, and they are seized everywhere, and taken to the Castle of Edinburgh.'

The minister in Colinton, the Revd George Gibson, only lived for a year after Culloden, and his successor, the Revd John Hyndman, had a fairly brief ministry in the parish, being translated to St Cuthbert's in Edinburgh in 1752. He was later to become a Moderator of the General Assembly. When he came to Colinton he found most of his parishioners still living in very meagre thatched houses of stone and lime, with small windows and damp, none-too-healthy earthen floors. They contrasted greatly with the grand mansions of the heritors in the neighbourhood.

The staple diet of the parishioners was also very different from the fare offered in the dining-rooms of Colinton Castle, Redhall or Woodhall. The villagers had porridge, oaten bread, milk, butter and cheese, and were getting more meat than their fathers had had. Some were even drinking tea, and trying out that strange vegetable called potatoes which were being grown out at Currie and Ratho – but in general the food was fairly monotonous.

Clothes, too, continued to be homespun. In the village street the women were to be seen wearing red plaids and cloth caps, sometimes decked with ribbons, gowns, petticoats and stockings which they had knitted themselves. The menfolk wore woollen bonnets, and coarsely-woven coats, waistcoats and breeches.

John Hyndman managed to leave the parish before the problem of the church fabric reached crisis level, and it was the Revd Robert Fisher, newly arrived from Lauder, who had to cope. It was becoming increasingly obvious that something drastic had to be done about the building, but the heritors, who would have to foot the bill, were unwilling to face up to reality.

In 1767 the farm of Mr James Gillespie in the parish of Colinton was surveyed by H Leslie, and on the site of the parish church in his map is a thumbnail sketch of a building. It is not shown in the conventional map-maker's way of a tower with a cross on the top, but seems to be representing an individual building with a bell tower. This may well be the earliest drawing which exists of Colinton Parish Church, and if so, it is easy to picture the anxious heritors inspecting its tower and walls in 1760.

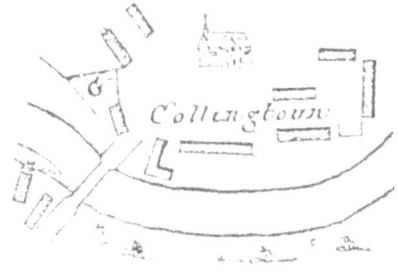

The Heritors' Records show that among other things 'the Kirk windows are in a ruinous condition', the minister's barn needed to be repaired, and that 'the planks above Woodhall Isle whereupon a part of the roof is supported are endangered by the rain getting in upon the flanks'. Estimates for these repairs came to £7.10.4d.

Four years later things had become worse. Two of the skylights in the body of the church were insufficient and needed to be repaired, as did the roofs of several aisles. Rain was coming into the church through the hole for the bellrope, and so the bellrope was moved to hang down the outside of the west wall. These stop-gap measures were clearly not enough, and by 1770 the heritors were sufficiently concerned to get an architect's opinion on the building. Messrs James Robertson and Alexander Gowan, Architects in Edinburgh, gave this alarming report:

Having narrowly inspected the Parish Church of Collintoun we found the whole of the side walls of the church hanging over, and having plumbed several parts of these walls, found them hanging over 13 inches at the height of 14 feet.

We found the East Gable rent from top to bottom, and greatly hanging over, and having pierced the walls both outside and inside the same appeared as if they were built with drystone and bedded with old lime rubbish, having no bond whatever.

The roof next the side walls will be found much decayed as it falls in too suddenly in such a manner that the water could not run off freely. That the said church is in such a ruinous condition that no repairs whatever can secure the safety thereof to the people who frequent the same to Divine Worship. We find the said church totally ruinous and dangerous and are of the opinion that the same ought to be taken down and rebuilt.

It is to be wondered that Mr Fisher ever entered his church again after reading this report, but apparently both he and his parishioners did, for the heritors were reluctant to face facts. However, in January 1771, they at least gave consideration to the building of a new church, and advertised in the *Edinburgh Evening Courant* as follows:

As the Heritors of Collingtoun Parish Church have a view of building a new church, the area to be fourteen hundred feet, the side walls sixteen feet high and the gable walls in proportion, any person willing to contract for building the same is desired to give in a plan and estimate thereof to Sir James Foulis of Colinton or to James Carmichael of Haills, as soon as possible, before the 1st of March next, the Contractor to be allowed all the old materials of the old church.

In March they met again and looked at six plans which had been submitted, the cheapest of which was to cost £260, including the old materials. The price must have given them cold feet, for after going over from the manse to the church to have another look at it, they decided that considering 'a most sufficient roof' had been put on within the last twenty years there was no need to build a new church – the old one could be repaired at a cost not exceeding £80. That was in March. A silence in the records of the next two months hides what must have been some hectic lobbying on the part of the minister, the elders and the parishioners about the state of their church, and a brief note on 3rd May 1771 of a heritors' meeting in John's Coffee House, Edinburgh, shows who won: 'The meeting resolves that the present church be taken down and a new church built on the same place.'

Robert Weir, the mason, and Walter Watters, wright, won the contract to build a church of squared rubble stone walls, not harled, and with a slated roof.

Twelve days later, Mr Foulis of Woodhall consented to let his Isle be taken down for the convenience of the parish. 'The Heritors shall pay him for the materials, and he shall have preferable choice of a loft, to be erected at common expense, also an area in the churchyard for a burying place, equal to the area of his isle.'

The heritors must have been relieved that they did not have to bear all the cost of the new building, which was to come to £322.10s.4d, for several farmers in the area offered subscriptions. After this, they did not waste much time, and by 1772, when it was nearly completed, they were meeting to apportion out the seating of the new church and decide upon its decoration. The fronts of the lofts, pulpit and precenter's desk were to be painted in a mahogany colour, and hung with green fringed cloth, and the posts supporting the gallery were to be painted green. By March 1773, Mr Fisher was able to preach in his new church, and the congregation worshipped again without fear of the roof falling in on top of their heads.

CHAPTER 8
Smuggling at Spylaw

BY the end of the eighteenth century, Colinton had for all time ceased to be a community of small settlements whose inhabitants relied solely on farming for a living. Even the old name of Hailes had virtually disappeared from all formal documents. The large estates which flourished in the parish gave employment to many of the local men and women, but the area where there was greatest expansion was on the Water of Leith. When the new church was being built in the Dell, that work-horse of a river was driving 71 mills, 16 of them being in Colinton parish providing work for 92 people.

Little relieved the daily drudgery of the mill-workers, but there certainly would have been a spark of excitement when news leaked out of skulduggery afoot at Upper Spylaw. William Reid, the owner of Upper Spylaw Mill, had invented and installed

IN 1773 JAMES GILLESPIE BUILT THIS HOUSE AT SPYLAW, HARNESSING THE WATER OF LEITH BEHIND IT FOR HIS MILL.

machinery at his snuff mill which manufactured the tobacco into snuff more quickly and cheaply than his competitors. The process, he insisted, had to be kept secret. However, it was rumoured that the workers at the rival snuff-mill of James Gillespie downstream at Spylaw had other ideas.

Four Excise officers and a constable, together with a smith and two wrights as assistants, raided the mill on the pretext of searching for smuggled goods. No contraband was found and the incensed Mr Reid was convinced the whole thing was a ruse to discover the secret of his machinery. As he pointed out in an angry petition to the Lords of Council and Session, the officers' 'assistants' were all skilled workmen familiar with mill machinery, and they were employed at Mr Gillespie's snuff-mill nearby.

The doings at Upper Spylaw were again the talk of the taverns a few years later, when it became known that the top storey of the mill was a hideout for smugglers. This time the customs raid was certainly genuine, for it was reported in the *Edinburgh Advertiser* of 30th April 1776, that the officers had seized from the mill 'sixteen chests and twenty bags containing about 2500 pounds weight of green and Bohea tea, and 3 anchors of brandy'. Whether the smugglers managed to escape over the Pentlands or down to the sea is not reported.

The Colinton mills were a steady source of employment. Their managers were versatile, and changed the products which were milled to suit the market. Sometimes the mills were used for waulking – the fulling and shrinking of cloth into thick and felted material; at other times they worked flax into linen, or ground barley, snuff or spices. At the Newmills Barley Mill belonging to Woodhall, a contemporary source recorded that the barley meal was ground and sent to Glasgow to be 'exported to the West Indies where it serves for the food of the negroes, the carts returning from Glasgow, loaded with rum and sugar'. One of the main products of the parish was paper, which was made as early as 1682 by James Lithgow at Spylaw. James Lithgow seems to have flirted with a little industrial malpractice, for he was accused by Alexander Daes of Dalry Paper Mill of secretly getting a licence for the manufacture of playing cards, and enticing away one of his workmen who had expertise in that field.

The lairds of Colinton, therefore, could not only buy playing cards which were made locally, but could also pay for their losses at cards with bank notes which were printed on paper manufactured in the parish. The Bank of Scotland had its twenty shilling banknotes manufactured at Boag's Mill in 1735, and security arrangements were strict during production times. The employees were given all their meals during the twelve day papermaking spell – mutton, chicken, duck, solan goose, eggs, cheese and bacon. Did they also sleep at the mill for security reasons?

By 1769 the paper for banknotes was being made at Redhall Mill and it appears that during the process the bank directors had a pleasant holiday in Colinton, ostensibly supervising the use of the frames for the notes. At the mill house they had 'a large

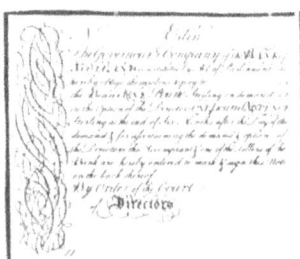

room fitted up to serve as a dining room for the bank directors, when occasion required, with a room adjoining used as a butler's pantry, and on the ground floor of the old mill there was a commodious kitchen, with an oven'.

The manufacture of paper was a prosperous occupation for the mill-owners, and they sometimes enlarged or rebuilt the mills to cope with the production. Kate's Mill, which had previously been known as the Waulk Mill of Colinton, was pulled down and rebuilt in 1787 'for the better accommodation of their paper manufactory'. The rent for the new mill was fixed at £13 and one ream of the best and finest writing-paper, and the mill-house on the bank above it was built with excellent cellars to house the wine needed for entertaining the bank directors when they came visiting. Folklore has it that Kate's Mill was named after the tenant's wife, Catherine Cant of Thruston. The nearby mill of Lumsdain's also had a change of name: when it was rebuilt in 1714 it became known by the far more intriguing name of Jinkabout.

Colinton at this time must have been an extremely noisy place in which to live, the constant clank of the mills drowning out any notion of peace and quiet along the river valley. One of the worst affected inhabitants must have been the minister, who lived

REDHALL MILL

with the Kirkland Mill on one side of the manse and the Hole Mill on the other.

Over at Longstone, however, a different noise began to assail the parish, that of a new-fangled steam engine which was installed in Hailes quarry to pump the water out. The opening of this quarry in 1750 brought work to 150 men who were to hew the stone which was used to build the first Royal Infirmary. In the next century, when the New Town was built, Hailes quarry was to yield six hundred carts of stone a day, all rumbling noisily from the northern boundary of the parish into the town.

Farming of course continued to occupy many of the parishioners, but here, too, there were changes from the old days. The lands were being enclosed and the run-rig system of farming was disappearing for good.

Sometimes the landowners' instructions for enclosure were very precise. When David Wright got his tack in 1744 for the lands of Caldhame, also known as Graysmill, it was laid down that he was under an obligation before 1756 to enclose the lands let 'with a ditch and hedge, the ditch to be six quarters wide at the surface, and five quarters in depth'. The areas enclosed were not to be larger than twelve acres or smaller than six. He was also bound 'to plant the outer and dividing ditches of the whole enclosures with thorn hedges and to put proper gates upon every enclosure, and likewise to plant thereon such barren timber as the proprietor shall direct by way of hedgerow, leaving twelve feet distance between every tree'.

The enclosure of an estate was considered an asset to it. In 1776, when the *Edinburgh Advertiser* printed an advertisement for the sale of Redford, Gallolee and Little Fordel, it stated that 'the land consisted of 100 acres Scots, all enclosed and properly sub-divided with strips of planting in a thriving condition, a great part of which is ready for cutting'.

The digging of ditches and planting of hedges was an expensive and time-consuming business, and when the enclosures were completed the owners protected them fiercely. In 1762 James Watson of Saughton, George Inglis of Redhall and James Carmichael of Hailes even went to court with a case against the Earl of Errol and the other members of the Edinburgh Hunt, so incensed were they at the hunt for breaking down their ditches and hedges, and riding through the grain. The rejoicing in the neighbourhood must have been great when the local lairds won their case.

The whole appearance of the parish altered with the enclosures. What had once been a bleak tract of moor, often boggy in places, became drained and cultivated, and green with the young trees which the owners were now keen to plant, not only for enclosure purposes, but for their attractive appearance. The cedars at Merchiston were raised from seed sent home from Aleppo, the balsam poplar at Craiglockhart planted around 1770 grew from seed brought home from the new colony of Canada. The holly hedges at Colinton Castle were now about a hundred years old and flourishing, and the landowners of Redhall, Hailes and Redford put similar hedges in their new gardens. The elms, beeches and alders planted at the beginning of the century by Sir John Foulis at Woodhall were now well established, and Mr Henry Trotter of Mortonhall began to clothe the Pentlands above Swanston with his plantations. The T-Wood dates from this time. (It is commonly supposed that this was planted as a self-assertive T for Trotter, because from Edinburgh the wood looks T-shaped, but in fact it is in the form of a Maltese Cross.) All in all, Scotland was becoming a greener place. Dr Samuel Johnson would no longer be able to make the scathing comment that a tree in Scotland was as rare a sight as a horse in Venice.

Estate gardens, too, were now to become an important feature of the parish, and they would provide work for the villagers. Henry Mackenzie, in his *Anecdotes and Egotisms* of the 1820s, wrote:

> *The science of gardening seems to have been successfully cultivated in the county of Edinburgh long ago. I forget at what period (I believe about the close of the seventeenth century) a treatise on gardening was published by the gardener at Colintoun, three miles from Edinburgh, which I have seen, and was thought to be a very sensible performance. Colintoun was then the property of the family of Fowlis, at that time possessed of very extensive property, whose gardener therefore was one of eminence.*
>
> *Some remains of his improvements remained till after I had attained the age of manhood. I remember being sent by a lady who then followed the fashionable amusement of breeding silk-worms, to Colintoun to get mulberry leaves, that being the only place in Scotland where mulberry trees were known to exist. Yet I recollect one solitary mulberry tree in my grandfather's garden at Nairn, from which, in favourable seasons, I have eaten ripe mulberries, which stood, I think, tho' a withered stump, yet now and then bearing a little fruit till within twenty or thirty years ago.*

The treatise Henry Mackenzie referred to may well be *The Scots Gardener* by John Reid, which was published in 1683. In 1779, however, another gardening book came out, *The Scotch Forcing Gardener* by Walter Nicol, who had been gardener at Wemyss Castle before moving to Leith to become an adviser on gardening. Lairds such as Lord Colinton consulted Walter Nicol's book, and the layout of the garden for the new Colinton House, which was built in the grounds of Colinton Castle in 1801, may well have come from its pages.

Walter Nicol tells his readers exactly how to manage the greenhouse and the heated walls of the garden. He advises on how to grow asparagus, cucumbers, cherries, grapes, melons, mushrooms, nectarines, peaches and strawberries. The diet of the landed gentry was becoming more and more varied, even exotic, and the people, too, had changes in their food. It became common now to have potatoes, cabbages, carrots and turnips – turnips were grown at Ratho and Currie for the first time in 1793 – and, much to the dismay of ministers and lairds, the 'pernicious habit' of drinking tea took root. 'A demoralising drug' was how the cup of tea was described by those who feared its powers.

No walled gardens, no greenhouses, however, could protect the crops and fruits from the winter of 1785, when exceptional snowfalls were recorded in Colinton starting on 14th January and continuing until the 18th March. The snow lay to an even depth of 38 inches, and the total snowfall that winter, which was carefully measured, amounted to $66^{1}/_{2}$ inches. On 23rd January, at 2 a.m., the temperature fell to 2 degrees Fahrenheit (minus 16 degrees Centigrade). With fuel constantly in short supply, the suffering in the village that winter must have been considerable.

With the sweeping changes in agricultural practices at the end of the eighteenth century, Colinton lost its cottar-folk, and instead acquired on the one hand tenant-farmers, who had some capital, and on the other hand farm labourers, who had little money and no land. Many farmers, however, allowed the married farm labourer to keep a cow and have a plot for growing his own vegetables and flax. As with his forbears, he was still paid partly in kind, but the oatmeal he received kept starvation from the door. Now he had a best dress, and when he went down The Row to kirk on a Sunday he wore a cloth coat, velvet waistcoat, breeches and calf-skin shoes. His shirt might have ruffles and his cravat be muslin. His womenfolk would appear in pretty cotton dresses, white stockings and carefully trimmed bonnets.

THE SEXTON – ALWAYS READY TO EXCHANGE THE NEWS

Perhaps the families stepped out on a Sunday brightly attired because attending church was becoming a much less awesome experience. By now the church's power of discipline had begun to wane and appearances at the repentance pillar ceased. Fines were no longer imposed for irregular marriages, which were marriages conducted by episcopal clergy without the tedious preliminaries of the 'Testificates' and other paperwork demanded by the Church of Scotland. Punishments were now only meted out to those who had sinned within the parish, not to those who lived in Colinton but had sinned elsewhere. Easier travel made it difficult for the Session to control the movements of people by the issue or refusal of a 'Testificate', and the whole attitude of the congregation towards the discipline of the Session was changing. By now the parish had as its incumbent a man whose religious fervour went hand in hand with the study of nature. By now the parish had the 'Mad Minister of Moffat'.

Dr John Walker's arrival in the parish caused a great furore – so great that there was even a local Secession and the Slateford Church was built as a result. A mild man by all accounts, he succeeded the Revd Robert Fisher, who died while minister of the parish in 1782, and who was buried by the south wall of the church 'loved and lamented by his friends and parishioners'.

One of the problems about Dr Walker was that he was not only a keen botanist, but sufficiently respected in this field to be made the first Professor of Natural History at the University of Edinburgh. This appointment he was determined to keep, as well as that of minister of the Church of Scotland. The other burden which Dr Walker had to bear was that he was foisted on the congregation by the patronage of Lord Lauderdale, whose estate at Hatton in West Lothian carried the patronage of Colinton Kirk. Lay Patronage had been reintroduced in 1712. For reasons of his own, the earl was bent on a ministerial shuffle. He offered a Mr Girvan to Colinton upon Mr Fisher's death, but there was such opposition from the people of Colinton to this appointment that even the Earl of Lauderdale had to

listen. Mr Girvan was dispatched to Moffat instead. The minister of Moffat, Dr Walker, was then transferred by Lord Lauderdale to Colinton, whether the congregation wanted him or not.

Coping with this highly charged situation was the interim moderator, the Revd Robert Walker of Cramond Kirk. Son of the Revd William Walker who had been minister at the Scots Kirk in Rotterdam, Robert spent some of his boyhood in Holland and had skated the Dutch canals. The year after Dr John Walker's appointment to Colinton, Robert Walker was transferred from Cramond to Canongate Kirk, very convenient for his favourite pastime – skating on Duddingston Loch. One of the most famous paintings in the National Gallery of Scotland, attributed to Henry Raeburn, depicts Revd Robert Walker skating on Duddingston Loch, arms folded Dutch fashion, in the hard winter of 1784. It seems clear from the serenity of the painting that he had put behind him the problems of his interim-moderatorship at Colinton.

REVD ROBERT WALKER SKATING ON DUDDINGSTON LOCH, BY HENRY RAEBURN
(*by courtesy of the National Gallery of Scotland*)

KIRK SESSION MINUTES – 5TH JANUARY 1703

The troubles of poor Dr John Walker, however, were only beginning. One parishioner said: 'He spends the week hunting butterflies and makes the cure of the souls of his parishioners a bye-job on Sunday.' Others, especially the women, suspected that he walked about on his rambles carrying curling tongs for his wig – it was in fact his insect net sticking out of his pocket. His depth of intelligence and commitment was not then appreciated in Colinton – he had at one time made journeys of 3000 miles in seven months on a commission from the General Assembly and the Society for the Propagation of Christian Knowledge to report on the state of affairs in the Hebrides – but parishioners did however marvel at the wide variety of plants he put into the manse garden.

Dr Walker also agitated for a new manse. On the very first day of his ministry, Sunday 27th February 1783, he called a meeting of the heritors and told them that the manse was so dilapidated that it would not do. There followed much acrimony among the heritors, who preferred the option of renovating to rebuilding, and the minister, who did not like housing his family in a manse where, according to one builder, the entire front wall and south gable needed to be taken down and the dining-room was so damp that the hearth needed to be drained.

Other contractors were consulted, and one, William Hill, reported that all the discrepancies in the walls could be made good and the manse made more cheerful and airy by enlarging the windows in the west wall, and 'at a much cheaper rate than any other person'. He also proposed that a drain should be dug on the west and north end of the manse 'which will be but a trifling expense and obviates any objection that may be made on account of the best room being a step or two below the surfaces of the external ground, in the same manner as was done at the mansion houses of Dreghorn and Redford'.

In the end the heritors unwillingly agreed to build a new manse, and entered into a contract with Robert Weir, mason, and Thomas Jack, wright, to demolish the old manse and build a new one of nearly the same dimensions. But apparently it was a pretty shoddy job, because Dr Walker complained of the poor standard of joinery work and various other things until two years later the heritors wearily asked him what it would take to make the manse 'agreeable' to him. The reply was: '£37', and pencilled in the margin of the heritors' minutes is 'and harling the walls'.

This was not quite the end of the story of the new manse. When Dr Walker wrote his contribution for the *First Statistical Account* in 1794, he penned:

> *The manse was built anno 1784, at an expense sufficiently liberal but with very insufficient workmanship. This is the case with the generality of manses in Scotland which renders them, in proportion to their size, the most expensive houses in the kingdom. Imperfectly executed at first, and that usually for want of a proper superintendence, their frequent repairs and rebuilding come to be a matter of great inconvenience to the incumbents and of much additional and unnecessary expense to the heritors.*

So as the parish moved into the new century, it had a church which was just thirty years old, a new manse of questionable workmanship with a new barn which had been made out of the old schoolhouse, and a new United Secession Church at Slateford, thanks to the overbearing behaviour of the Earl of Lauderdale.

The roads in the village had been mapped by Roy in the 1750s and again by Laurie in 1786. Penal laws against Episcopalians had been abolished and the Relief Act for Catholics had been passed. The population of Colinton stood roughly at 1397, but peaceful times for the villagers did not lie ahead. Some of the young men were soon to die fighting on the fields of Spain and France or in the great sea battles of Nelson. War had been declared between Napoleon's France and Great Britain and, as of old, Colinton people left home to follow the colours. Captain John Inglis of Redhall was commissioned to the Coromandel, a ship of 24 guns – he raised 79 men to go with him. Many from his own neighbourhood followed him to Leith, and many did not return.

CHAPTER 9

The National Roll-Calls

WHEN the minister of the parish, Dr John Walker, was not busy complaining about his new manse, or teaching his students at Edinburgh University, or seeing to his parish duties with his butterfly net tucked into his pocket, he was gathering material for his contribution on Colinton for the *Statistical Account of Scotland*. He had been asked to do this by Sir John Sinclair of Ulbster, who was masterminding this extraordinarily imaginative survey of the life and times of Scotland in the 1790s, parish by parish.

The object of the survey was not 'statistical' as we think of it, but rather, in Sir John Sinclair's words, an 'enquiry into the state of a country for the purpose of ascertaining the quantum of happiness enjoyed by its inhabitants and means of its future improvement'. To this end a list of queries was sent to every parish minister in Scotland, and many co-operated with enthusiasm in giving their replies.

In his report the minister of Penicuik wrote: 'The people are of various sizes. They are like those of other parishes, many of them good and some of them bad.' How did Dr Walker evaluate his parishioners? What 'quantum of happiness' did he find among the Colinton people in 1794? He wrote of a parish of 5000 Scots acres, of mills, quarries, woods, plantations and enclosed lands, making it 'one of the most productive parts of the country'. People found employment in farming and the mills where they ground flour and barley, manufactured paper, lint and tobacco, and waulked cloth. They also worked in the skinnery, at the bleaching fields of the private estates and of Inglis Green, in the magnesia factory and the 'flourishing distillery' at Bow Bridge. The quarries of Redhall and Hailes gave many men employment.

But whereas there seem to have been opportunities for improving one's standard of living in the village, there was little for the incumbent in the manse. The minister's stipend in 1792 was the same as it was in 1635. Dr Walker observed testily: 'The fall of money in its value is well known to be a great hardship, and especially of late, upon all persons of a fixed income, and upon none more than upon the clergy of Scotland.'

His glebe did not please him either: 'The extent of the glebe is less than what the law appoints; but even though it were of legal size, it could not be profitably occupied and cultivated by the incumbent, without an opportunity of renting so much additional land as would afford sufficient work for a man-servant and two horses.'

The parish school did, on the other hand, meet with Dr Walker's approval: 'It has always been well taught, and well attended, not only by children of the middle and lower ranks, but many gentlemen, who have afterwards proved an honour to their country, have received the elements of their education here.' He felt that the schoolmaster's salary was not, however, enough to induce a well qualified young man to take the post.

The church looked after the poor of the parish by giving them a monthly allowance – but it was on condition that they did not beg: 'There are no beggars belonging to the parish, as it is made known to all who are admitted upon the poors-roll, that if they happen to beg they forfeit their pension.'

In the fields now there were oats, wheat, barley, beans, pease, clover and rye-grass. The cultivation of flax had declined, but there were extensive fields of potatoes and smaller quantities of turnips.

Wheat had become the most profitable crop: 'A great deal of land, though naturally unfit for wheat, is, by the aid of the Edinburgh dung, employed in raising that grain.' The carts that brought the dung from Edinburgh to Colinton frequently returned to town full of corn, hay and straw. On the farms there were 171 work horses and 127 cows, and grazing on the Pentlands 4000 sheep. The number of winter hives of bees, however, had declined to 35. Ten carriage horses and 31 saddle horses took the gentry to and fro.

On population statistics, Dr Walker was similarly precise. He referred to the very first attempt at a national roll-call, that of the Revd Dr Alexander Webster, who in 1755 enlisted the help of ministers to compile his returns. The Webster census gave Colinton parish a population of 792. Dr Walker calculated that in 1794 there were 313 inhabited houses and 1395 people – the increase of 75 per cent in 39 years being due to the expansion of Edinburgh and of local manufacturing. The parish register revealed, however, that the rate of children dying under the age of 14 was still alarmingly high – on average nearly half of all those who died each year. This was in spite of Dr Walker's statement that 'there are no local distempers, nor any peculiar appearance of any disease observable in this parish. The air is salubrious, and the soil in general dry, without any ground fogs or stagnating water'. The parish burial records which give cause of death tell a different story.

While both the Webster and Sinclair Accounts were private enterprises, the first national census of 1801 was funded by the government. The crisis of the Napoleonic wars had made the government realise how important it was to take stock of the country's population and assets. At this early stage, statistics were not listed for age or even marital status, and it was not until 1841 that the census revealed information on the place of birth of people as well as their present residence. The first census in 1801, however, showed no change to Dr Walker's statistics – Colinton parish had a population of 1397, only two more than in his day. There were 302 inhabited houses and 31 uninhabited; the chief occupation was agricultural labouring – 161 people worked on the land, but the combined figure of 158 for those employed in trade, manufacturing and handicraft work showed that Colinton was no longer a purely rural area.

Gentlemen, however, still had fine estates at Colinton. At Craiglockhart there was Dr Alexander Monro *secundus*, son of the famous Dr Alexander Monro *primus*, who was the first Professor of Anatomy in Edinburgh. Dr Monro *secundus* passed on his own professorship and his estate to his son, Alexander *tertius*. Neither had lived in the old mansion house, but Alexander *tertius* decided he wanted to have a residence on the estate and he built

WHEN ALEXANDER TROTTER BOUGHT DREGHORN CASTLE IN 1799,
HE ENLARGED IT AND FURNISHED IT LAVISHLY.

Craiglockhart House, a modern dwelling nearer the Dell and lived many years in it.

To Dreghorn there came Alexander Trotter. Made rich by speculating public funds on his own behalf as Paymaster of the Navy, he bought Dreghorn Castle in 1799 which he then proceeded to enlarge and refurbish lavishly. Later he acquired the mansion of Kirklands which stood by the church and the bridge in the village. The lands of Little Fordel, Gallolee and Redford also came into his possession, and in addition more land from the impoverished Foulis family, and from James Forrest of Comiston.

With him came more new lairds to the parish, who set about building fine houses and altering the landscape with their grand estate plans. At Colinton Castle the final blow came to the branch of the Foulis family who had lived there since the sixteenth century – they had to sell off the Castle and its surrounding parks. Sir William Forbes, a successful banker in the town, who had married the first love of Sir Walter Scott, became the new owner, and he decided to build a more comfortable house for his home, a little to the north of the Castle.

Colinton House was begun in 1801, but Sir William did not live long enough to inhabit it – he died in 1806, and his heir, Sir William, did not wish to put down permanent roots there.

*To mark the 900th anniversary celebrations, the Lord
Lyon granted armorial bearings to Colinton Kirk.*

*Ethelred's charter of the land of Hailes no longer exists, but in the National Library of Scotland
there is a charter dated c. 1128 containing confirmation by David I of his brother's gift. The words
'Dona Ethelredi fris mei, Hale' – Hales, the gifts of my brother Ethelred – appear in the second column
of the vellum, lines thirteen and fourteen, and this is the first written evidence of the
foundation of the church of Hailes.*

The tomb of St Cuthbert, for long a place of pilgrimage, is in Durham Cathedral. It is still highly honoured.

The oldest surviving inscription in the church is the grave-marker of Agnes Heriot, dated 8 August 1593. On the 400th anniversary of her death it was garlanded.

Up to the late nineteenth century one of the duties of the elders was to stand at the Offertory House to collect the offering. Woe betide anyone who put a button in the plate.

The church, photographed in the time of Dr Laing, has altered little.

Baberton House, with its 1622 window, is the oldest intact domestic building in the original parish.

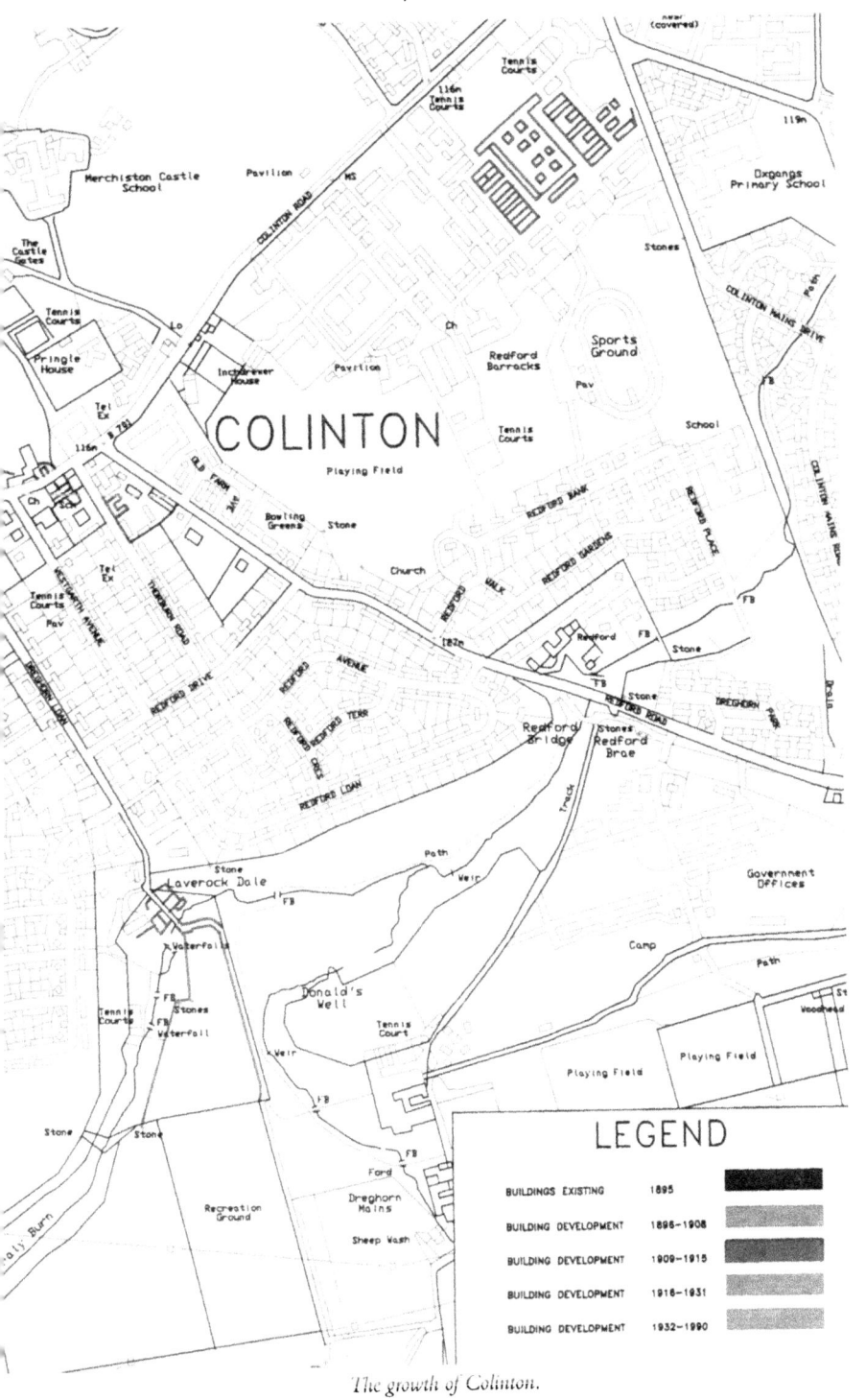

The growth of Colinton.

From earliest times the Water of Leith was the hub of Colinton Village.

Striking features of Colinton Parish Church are its cross-beam, distinctive pulpit and finely carved war memorial.

The Long Steps – originally the way to the ford.

Colinton Village.

The Kirk.

The Very Revd Dr W B Johnston in his Moderatorial Year.

Recent developments have spread Colinton from the Dell right out to the Pentland Hills.

Tucked into an elbow of land at the Water of Leith, the parish kirk and manse are at the heart of the Village.

Today's minister, the Revd George J Whyte, looks back over 900 years of history, but also looks forward.

He sold it to Lord Dunfermline who, upon his resignation as Speaker of the House of Commons, came to Colinton House. This building is now the science block of Merchiston Castle School, but the formal splendour of its plastered ceilings and well-proportioned rooms is evident to this day. In addition, the boys at the school, while working away at their Biology, still have a view of the ruins of Colinton Castle, which were battered into their present shape by a cannon which was brought up from Leith by Sir William Forbes, on the suggestion of the painter Alexander Nasmyth. Picturesque ruins in the garden were fashionable at the time.

Enough was left after the cannon balls, however, for the Victorians, and even present-day Elizabethans, to picture what the castle had been like. In 1902 David Shankie, in his book *The Parish of Colinton* wrote rather fancifully:

COLINTON FARM – SITE OF THE PRESENT-DAY OLD FARM COURT.

Crossing the low doorway one stands a few moments in the old kitchen, up the wide chimney of which, now black and cold, great fires once blazed and crackled. Then peep into the other rooms, long low, narrow, gloomy places, and after a moment or two turn away with a shudder. Ascending a narrow winding stair we are brought up to what would be the principal rooms, all arousing the interest and claiming the attention. From the large window in front we may gaze down on what was once the court-yard, and as we stand here in this deserted ruin the

95

present is for a time forgotten, fancy wanders back to the days when the old castle was the abode of the great and the gay; when the walls rang with sounds of mirth and revelry, and from its court-yard many a merry band rode forth to the tournament and the chase.

Shankie, like other writers, was intrigued by what was taken to be the remains of the family chapel. He described a ruined western gable, a few yards to the east of the great holly hedge which grows to this day. 'It has two little windows which have been described as "anries", from which would be distributed charities to the poor. This, however, cannot be as they are not out through the wall. They were more probably used for holding rosaries, *etc.*, used in the Roman Catholic form of worship.'

This gable wall also interested John Geddie, the author of *The Water of Leith, Source to Sea:* 'A forlorn and eerie, little scrap of ruin – a lowly gable wall with the dead trunk and skeleton limbs of an ivy tree twined around the staring window and "Open Door".' Both writers refer to the fact that Margaret Oliphant, when writing her famous Victorian ghost story, used this as the setting for her strange tale entitled *The Open Door.*

At the time of the first census, however, even less remained of the two other ancient fortalices of the parish than of Colinton Castle. Redhall had been a solid L-shaped building with a  circular stair tower at the north-east corner. It had a courtyard, offices, a cherry garden, an orchard and even a bowling green. But after Cromwell's devastation of 1650 it had become so ruinous that it was deemed valueless and demolished in 1755 by George Inglis when he built the new Redhall House in the style of a French chateau. He used the stones of the old castle for his building, but retained the sixteenth century Otterburn coat of arms, and incorporated them into his new hexagonal dovecote.

The other old fortalice, Craiglockhart Castle, was also unable to withstand the ravages of the elements, invasion and neglect. By 1691 a two-storey mansion house had replaced the tower and fortalice, and by the beginning of this century only a few tree-covered walls remained of the old building.

The war with Napoleon did not seem to affect the building programmes in Colinton, for they went on apace. The road from the Cockit Hat Plantation at the Hunter's Tryst to Redford and the village was built in 1802, and Sir James Forrest planned the new Comiston House the same year as Waterloo. The basic layout of today's parish roads began to take shape. Twelve people were employed to complete a road which ran between the Lanark Road and the Glasgow Road, and which became known as the 'Thieves' Road' because it provided an excellent getaway for highwaymen going about their business on the two main highways.

Perhaps the biggest development in the area was, contradictorily, a demolition – the destruction of Bonaly Village by Lord Cockburn when he decided make Bonaly his home.

In March 1811 I married, and set up my rural household gods at Bonaly, in the parish of Colinton, close to the northern base of the Pentland Hills; and unless some avenging angel shall expel me, I shall never leave that paradise. I began by an annual lease of a few square yards and a scarcely habitable farm-house: but realising the profanations of Auburn, I have destroyed a village, and erected a tower, and reached the dignity of a twenty-acred laird.

In Lord Cockburn's defence – though he does not seem to wish defence of his action – the Bonaly community was probably disintegrating before his arrival. The enclosures and improved farming methods had already caused drift from the land and more money could be earned elsewhere. There were still inhabited cottages around the old farmhouse which he bought, but there were probably deserted houses too.

D. O. HILL'S PHOTOGRAPH OF BONALY TOWER SHOWS IT AS COCKBURN BUILT IT. THE 17TH CENTURY FARMHOUSE (LEFT) IS STILL RECOGNISABLE. THE ADDITION OF A TURRETED LIBRARY WING IN 1888 MASKED THE ORIGINAL BUILDING.
(by courtesy of the Scottish National Portrait Gallery)

Before the 1888 addition of the library wing, it was possible to see the outline of the old farmhouse which was built *circa* 1650, and Cockburn's grand additions of rooms and a tower have made a building which now houses several households. In the garden is the only statue of Shakespeare to be found in Edinburgh. This was originally in Shakespeare Square in the centre of town, but put in the garden at Bonaly by Cockburn when the square was demolished.

Lord Cockburn had many of Edinburgh's *literati* out to Bonaly, and spoke with pride to his visitors about his rural life there. His shepherd, however, was not so impressed. When Cockburn said to him: 'John, if I were a sheep, I would lie on the sunny side of the hill', he replied: 'Ah, my Lord, but if ye was a sheep ye would hae mair sense.'

The minister, Dr Walker, who would have enjoyed talking to Cockburn about the ways of sheep and natural history in general, did not, however, live to see the great changes wrought at Bonaly. He died in 1803. During his long ministry at Colinton his parishioners became used to his eccentric ways, and the Church honoured him by making him Moderator of the General Assembly in 1790.

In the last years of his life he could no longer see the beautiful flower beds he had so lovingly laid out in the manse garden, for he became blind. It is as well he never knew what devastation the next incumbent, the Revd John Fleming, caused there – he yanked all the flowers out and planted rows of potatoes in their place. But then Mr Fleming was not only a minister, but a valuer of landed estates and a farmer. He had been at one time factor to the Earl of Rosebery, which is why, perhaps, he took a very professional interest in the fabric of the church and manse.

He, like his predecessor, did not think much of the new manse. In spite of it being just twenty years old, he wanted the whole edifice demolished and a new manse built across the road in the glebe. The heritors tried to postpone this calamity by voting £200 for improvements to the house in 1805, but Mr Fleming, still determined to get a new manse, stalled them until 1807, when he capitulated and allowed an addition to the building to be constructed. Nearly two hundred years on, this manse, in its leafy rural setting, still serves the parish.

ONE OF THE MORTSAFES, ACQUIRED BY COLINTON PARISH CHURCH TO THWART BODY-SNATCHERS OF THE BURKE AND HARE ERA, STILL SITS IN THE GRAVEYARD.

The heritors' expenses were not, however, over. In 1811 they resolved to build a new school 'on the bank south of the new street of the village', and a few years later the church roof was deemed to be unsafe. On this occasion they were not so tardy about their responsibilities and they hastily replaced the old roof, at the same time raising the walls of the church four feet so that the kirk acquired a loftier appearance.

In a few years they had another expense – the purchase of six mortsafes which had to be acquired to thwart the activities of the body-snatchers. When Burke and Hare were at the height of their grisly business of selling corpses, often stolen from new graves, to the Medical School for dissection, the old Session House at the gate of the church was used as a watch-house.

By the time John Fleming's ministry drew to a close, the country at large had seen many changes. The slave trade had been abolished, the Sutherland Clearances had begun, and Bell had built his revolutionary Comet steamship. In Colinton the children in the new school were now being taught English, writing, arithmetic, mensuration, book-keeping, Latin and the first prin-

ciples of Greek. When they walked home up Redford Road, or Woodhall Road, or over the river to the mill-houses down the Dell, they went to solid little houses of stone, slate-roofed and weatherproof, and ate meals of a far more varied diet than had ever been known previously.

Very occasionally they went into Edinburgh with their parents, along the new turnpike road past Firrhill and Craiglockhart, and in 1822 great would be the clamouring for such a trip, for this was the year of the first visit to Edinburgh of a Hanoverian king, George IV. How the tongues must have wagged in the inns in the village after a first extraordinary viewing of this ludicrous plump little king from the south, dressed in a ridiculously short kilt, woollen socks worn over pink stockings, and a feather bonnet. No one had ever seen anything like it, although Lady Hamilton-Dalrymple, one of the ladies attending the event, is said to have commented: 'Since he is to be among us for so short a time, the more we see of him the better.'

Certainly the gentry at Colinton did not wear such clothing. For outdoor excursions they wore breeches, tall boots, tail coats and embroidered waistcoats. Their ladies liked long full-skirted gowns in elegant fabrics, frilled at the hem, which they wore with lace fichus and intricately worked bonnets.

In the village the Colinton men went to their daily work in

heavy breeches or trousers, dun-coloured jackets and woollen shirts. Often the only colour to relieve their drab clothes was the scarlet or blue of the kerchief they wore round their necks. Through the week they wore bonnets, and for the fair and Sundays they had tall-crowned felt hats. The womenfolk had ankle-length skirts which they kilted up for work at the bleaching field or at the harvest, and brightly-coloured shawls. They did not feel correctly dressed without their mutches – little caps, often tied under the chin – which they wore both indoors and outdoors. Their minister, Dr Lewis Balfour, when writing on Colinton in the *Second Statistical Account* in 1838, had this to say about his parishioners' dress: 'The people are on the whole attentive to cleanliness, dress well on the Sabbath, and, if they would act aright, have the comforts and advantages of society in a reasonable degree.'

Future generations are apt to give recognition to Dr Lewis Balfour purely because he was the grandfather of Robert Louis Stevenson. In fact, Robert Louis was only ten years old when his grandfather died in the parish, and Dr Balfour's parishioners appreciated him for other reasons. Although rather daunting, he was much loved, particularly because of his compassion when carrying out his pastoral care. He was called to the parish upon the death of his predecessor, Revd John Fleming, in 1823, and clearly knew his people and district very well by the time he wrote his contribution to the *Statistical Account*. From it comes an excellent picture of Colinton in the early nineteenth century.

There were 16 mills and one bleach-field on the Water of Leith, but the river could not always be relied upon to be full enough to drive the wheels. On the other hand, there were sometimes disastrous flood-waters – in October 1832 there were three days of flooding during which twelve dam-heads were damaged and the bridge at Slateford, which had stood for seventy years, was brought down. Indeed there had been a proposal to have a reservoir to control the fickle Water of Leith, but the plan had never been carried out.

Dr Balfour recorded carefully the wildlife of the parish. There were kestrels breeding in the rocks at Craiglockhart, brown owls, the 'snowflake' which we know as the snow bunting, bramblings, the Bohemian chatterer (waxwing), long-tailed tits, gold crests, the 'butcher-bird' (red-backed shrike), ring-ousel, moorhens and the kingfisher, which it was thought on one occasion had had a nest near Slateford.

On its botany, the minister made particular reference to a small yellow poppy which appeared in the manse garden shortly after he had arrived there. It was said to be planted at Woodhall, but its normal habitat was the mountains of Wales. Today this yellow poppy grows in the parish like a weed.

As he went around his parish, Dr Balfour took note of the state of the plantations at Woodhall, Spylaw, Colinton House, Hailes, Redhall, Craiglockhart and Dreghorn, where Mr Trotter's trees were planted right up the Whitehill. The soft wood there, he saw, soon began to decay, while the hardwood, especially the ash and elm, continued to thrive. In good shape were the two large yews in the parish, the one in the manse garden and the one at Woodhall, as were the cedars of Lebanon at Colinton House. Dr Balfour himself was to plant exotic trees in the manse garden from seed sent home from abroad by his family.

In the 1831 Census, the population of the parish was 2232 people, but by the time Dr Balfour was writing seven years later it had decreased to 1982. He suggested that this was caused by the fact that the extra work on the farms of enclosure and hedging had been completed, that the quantity of stone being taken out of Hailes quarry had decreased and that Redhall quarry had ceased altogether to be worked. In addition, three of the paper mills were now using machinery, and therefore requiring fewer workers. Since the last *Statistical Account* the distillery had disappeared, the skinnery had gone from the Laverockdale area, and the magnesia factory was in ruins.

At that time the parish was still considered to be a collection of villages, hamlets and small knots of houses – it did not yet have the village suburb identity which came with the advent of the railway. Of the villages of Colinton, Swanston, Juniper Green, Hailes and Slateford, the largest was oddly enough not Colinton itself with 119 people, but Juniper Green with 338 inhabitants. One explanation for this may be that many of the quarriers lived there. Altogether there were 445 houses in the parish, and 52 uninhabited ones.

Dr Balfour was not uncritical of his flock. He noted with great regret that they were not 'given to reading' – the introduction of 'itinerating libraries' had failed because of lack of support. Even worse, however, was the parishioners' liking for liquor. 'One vice prevails greatly among the people, which eats out a man's heart, and renders him indifferent to religion, to knowledge, and to his nearest and dearest friends, *viz.* the drinking of ardent spirits.'

A Temperance Society had been founded in 1830 to educate the people about the consequences of their drinking, but 'the novelty of the thing wore off, the lover of drink returned to it again, and though the society still exists, its influence is little felt beyond the range of those who have conscientiously entered it; while the evil practice is spreading its influence even among the female part of our population'. Poor Dr Balfour. He had reason to have cause for concern – in 1832 there were 14 ale-houses in the parish. If these were located in the five villages, that comes to nearly three per village.

On the farms the practice was to rotate crops: first potatoes, turnips or beans, second wheat or barley; the third crop sewn was hay and the fourth oats. There were few cattle in the parish, and few sheep, except on the farms with land on the Pentlands. Cheviots abounded there, and on the hill of Craiglockhart there were a few Leicester sheep. The main crop was now potatoes.

Agricultural labourers continued to be paid in kind. A married ploughman, say on the farm at Swanston, would be paid £16 a year in cash, 65 stones of oatmeal, 12 cwt. of potatoes, and four weeks' food during harvest. He would also have a small thatched or tiled cottage and garden free, and coals.

Women and boys worked in the fields at hoeing for 9d a day, but at harvest time, their wages were regulated by the hiring market which was held in Edinburgh every Monday morning during the season. Among the labourers of the parish, the quarry men at Hailes earned the highest wages. Machinery was also beginning to displace workers on the farm. At Bonaly Steading a steam-engine had been installed by Gillespie's hospital, who owned the land, for driving the threshing-mill.

The pattern of employment was also altering for the older parishioners. Spinning in the cottages had almost disappeared.

'Thus the old are cut off from the employment, within the power of age and suited to its disposition, of "drawing out a thread wi' a little din"; which used to keep time from being a burden, and to supply the necessaries of life. There is but one weaver in the parish, whose work is not abundant.'

By Dr Balfour's time there were, as he called them, Dissenters, Episcopalians, Papists, Independents and Seceders of several varieties. For some of them their place of worship was in the town rather than in Colinton.

> *One great evil resulting from which is that, of necessity, they are left without pastoral superintendence, as sheep having no shepherd.*
>
> *It has, indeed, ever been the steady aim of the present incumbent to minister parochially. All within the bounds of his parish he considers as placed under his care, and, amid much weakness and imperfection, he extends his attentions to all who are willing to receive them. He has the satisfaction of adding that during the thirty-two years in which he has been allowed to be put in trust with the Gospel, he has met with uniform kindness from his parishioners, by whatever name they have been distinguished.*

Having said that, Dr Balfour had to convey that he was not uniformly impressed by the attendance at his church:

> *The church was long exceedingly ill attended in winter, its coldness being pleaded as an excuse. In summer it is well filled, but it must with sorrow be acknowledged, that the hurtful and unchristian practice of attending public worship in the forenoon only, too generally pervades all classes of society.*

The Colinton children, installed in their new school above the village, were ably taught by Mr Robert Hunter, who was qualified to teach English, writing, geometry, arithmetic, geography, Latin, Greek and French. But in spite of his obvious abilities he had to eke out his salary by being the postmaster of Colinton as well. In addition he was session clerk, clerk to the heritors and collector of the parochial assessments. He had between 90 and 100 pupils, so he was clearly a busy man.

Besides the parochial school there were six private schools in the parish, but Dr Balfour was not overly enthusiastic about them: 'In these schools English and writing are taught, and in two a little arithmetic is added.' The parish children were not short of religious instruction, however. There were five Sabbath-evening schools, one in each of the principal villages, and a tract called *The Monthly Visitor* was left with all 440 families each month.

In those times there was no State help when the breadwinner in a family fell ill, although the church did its best to look after the poor by diverting funds to them raised from the collection, from mortcloth dues and marriage fees, after the necessary church expenses had been met. Dr Balfour, though, was impatient of some of the families who received this cash: 'The people are not unwilling to receive parochial aid, and many would rather leave their relatives a burden on the public, than lessen in the least their own comforts. But to this there are honourable exceptions.'

Not all Colinton people were unable or unprepared to cater for bad times, however. There were two Friendly Societies in the parish which strove to help their members in time of need.

Such times were aplenty. Death in a family was never far away. Consumption claimed many, and epidemic diseases like scarlet fever were frequently rampant with little medicine to combat them. Measles, smallpox, cholera, typhoid and influenza were all too often fatal, especially among the young. Sometimes whole families of children were wiped out within a few weeks.

A disease called 'chincough' (a form of whooping cough) took many infant lives, and in older people the cause of death was often listed as 'water of the chest', 'water of the head', 'dropsy', and 'putrid sore throat'. Stillbirths and accidents occurred all too often. The parish burial records make sad reading. Indeed it is surprising that, despite frequent tragedies, the people kept a sense of humour – look at the pithy inscription on the stone of Slateford weaver, William Niven, who died on 11th April 1791:

> *Death's a debt*
> *To nature deeu*
> *I have paid her*
> *So mon you.*

CHAPTER 10

Robert Louis Stevenson Slept Here

On the forenoon of the second day, coming to the top of a hill, I saw all the country fall away before me down to the sea; and in the midst of this descent, on a long ridge, the city of Edinburgh smoking like a kiln. There was a flag upon the castle, and ships moving or lying anchored in the firth; both of which, for as far away as they were, I could distinguish clearly; and both brought my country heart into my mouth.

Presently after, I came by a house where a shepherd lived, and got a rough direction for the neighbourhood of Cramond; and so, from one to another, worked my way to the westward of the capital by Colinton, till I came out upon the Glasgow road.

THUS Robert Louis Stevenson, writing in Bournemouth, directed David Balfour in Kidnapped, when the boy made his fateful journey down to Cramond and the house of Shaws. How did Davie pass through Colinton? Did he take the road from the Hunters' Tryst south of the Dreghorn Estate and down past Laverockdale to Dreghorn Loan and the Long Steps? Or did he branch right at the Hunters' Tryst to where the Cockit Hat Plantation now grows, and reach the village by the Colinton Mains farm? Probably he went the way R.L.S. used to go when he stayed at Swanston Cottage, the family's country retreat from Heriot Row – down from Swanston, through the Burn Parks and Limey Lands, Sourhole and Trench Knowe Park, to Oxgangs Road, then past the cottages at Baads and Fordel,

ROBERT LOUIS STEVENSON'S SIGNATURE
– NOW PRESERVED IN OXGANGS PRIMARY SCHOOL.

and finally by the old white house of Redford and the fields of Colinton Farm, to the Dell.

Robert Louis was christened Robert Lewis Balfour Stevenson, the middle names being after his maternal grandfather, Revd Lewis Balfour, minister at Colinton. Dr Balfour christened the baby at his home, 8 Howard Place, Edinburgh, and there exists in the *Beinecke Collection of Letters* at the University of Yale in America, a letter to the Stevensons from Dr Balfour headed Colinton manse and dated the 10th of December 1850, which states: 'Jane and I will have much pleasure in being with you on Friday at 1 o'clock. I have not the smallest objection to the name you give the boy.' Whether Dr Balfour took with him for this very special family occasion the pewter baptism basin which he used at Colinton and is still owned by the church, or whether he used a receptacle from the Howard Place kitchen, is not on record.

PHOTOGRAPH OF R. L. STEVENSON TAKEN IN SAMOA, FOUND RECENTLY IN A COLLECTION OF GLASS PLATES IN THE CHURCH HALL.

Curiously, the child's mother Margaret Isabella, who kept a baby book of this much loved baby charting meticulously his first sounds and steps, left the Baptism page completely blank. She merely recorded later that his first journey was to Colinton manse when he was three months old.

In his late teens Robert Lewis changed the spelling to Louis. One story is that his father, a dyed-in-the-wool Tory, took issue with a Radical member of the Town Council called Lewis. Another is that his mother preferred Louis. Interestingly she used that spelling in the baby book she began when he was a few months old. On the Birth page she wrote firmly: 'Surname: Stevenson. Christian Names: Robert Louis Balfour.'

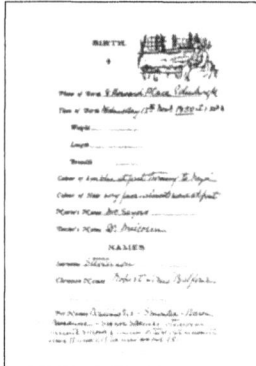

However, the version of his cousin, Graham Balfour, in his *Life of Robert Louis Stevenson*, is that the boy used to sign himself 'R. Stevenson' until he was 15 years old, then after that occasionally 'R.L.B. Stevenson'. When he was 18 years old, however, he asked his mother to address him as Robert *Lewis* instead of 'R.L.B. Stevenson'. The change of spelling to Louis came very shortly after this. The Balfour he finally dropped in about 1873 when he wrote in a letter: 'After several years of feeble and ineffectual endeavour with regard to my third initial (a thing I loathe) I have been led to put myself out of reach of such accident in future by taking my first two names in full.' But neither he, nor his family, nor his close friends, ever changed the pronunciation of Louis to the French form. Many simply called him 'Lou'.

Whatever the reason for the change, and the 'loathing' of the third initial, there was never any indication that R.L.S. disliked his Balfour grandfather. He was just ten years old when his grandfather died, but his memories of his days at the manse, where he was often brought from town to recuperate from the bouts of illness caused by a weakness in his lungs, remained vividly with him till his death in 1894 in Samoa.

In the rambling manse, Lewis Balfour and his wife Henrietta raised a large family, including the mother of R.L.S. – Margaret Isabella. So many of these children eventually scattered to all corners of the world to make their mark that R.L.S. was to write of his aunts and uncles: 'The face of the earth was peppered with the children of the manse, and letters with outlandish stamps became familiar to the local postman.'

THE REVD LEWIS BALFOUR

Of the manse, he was to remember with particular affection the water door in the garden:

The river is there dammed back for the service of the flour-mill just below, so that it lies deep and darkling, and the sand slopes into brown obscurity with a glint of gold; and it has but newly been recruited by the borrowings of the snuff-mill just above, and these, tumbling merrily in, shake the pool to its black heart, fill it with drowsy eddies, and set the curded froth of many other mills solemnly steering to and fro upon the surface.

Or so it was when I was young; for change, and the masons, and the pruning-knife, have been busy; and if I could hope to repeat a cherished experience, it must be on many and impossible conditions ....

It was a place in that time like no other: the garden cut into provinces by a great hedge of beech, and over-looked by the church and the terrace of the churchyard, where the tombstones were thick, and after nightfall 'spunkies' might be seen to dance, at least by children; flower-pots lying warm in sunshine; laurels and the great yew making elsewhere a pleasing horror of shade; the smell of water rising from all round, with an added tang of paper-mills; the sound of water everywhere, and the sound of mills – the wheel and the dam singing their alternate strain; the birds on every bush and from every corner of the overhanging woods pealing out their notes until the air throbbed with them; and in the midst of this, the manse.

I see it, by the standard of my childish stature, as a great and roomy house. In truth, it was not so large as I supposed, nor yet so convenient, and, standing where it did, it is difficult to suppose that it was healthful ....

Yet it was a homely house. In the time of the childhood of R.L.S., roses climbed up the side walls, and an espalier plum spread its branches over the front of the house. In the garden there was a glossy semi-circle of laurels crowned by a huge lilac tree which fringed the sloping lawn. Dr Balfour, when he was not busy in his study with what his grandson called his 'bloodless books', had spent many an hour improving the garden. When he had taken over from the Revd John Fleming, he had found a profusion of weeds, a few marigolds, the big old yew, an apple tree and not much else. The potatoes which Mr Fleming had so enthusiastically planted when he had come to the parish were no longer in evidence. Lewis and Henrietta planned to rear their large family in a cheerful garden of flowers and lawns.

Henrietta also had well defined ideas of how her household should be run. When she was writing to Margaret McKerrow in 1843, a young servant from Ayrshire applying to work as a kitchen servant in the manse, she penned:

The great point in our service is perfect cleanliness, and never to leave anything dirty or out of place. I am also particular in having my work done in my own way and in my own time. Nothing unreasonable will be asked or expected.

Besides the kitchen work, you will have the under flat of the house to keep clean (except the dining-room), the servants' room, and the outdoor places; the hens to feed and the hen-house to keep perfectly clean; kitchen floors, coal-house, well-trough, etc.. Of course there are many little particulars which it is impossible to specify in a letter, but I may mention a few of them – assisting to make the beds, clean the shoes, etc..

Mr Dalgleish mentions that you think the wages small, but ten shillings more in the half year is the highest I have given since I had a nursery-maid, and as I will have your travelling expenses to pay I cannot promise you more than the three pounds for this half-year. However, if you study to please me, be sober-minded, honest, obliging and willing to do all you can to serve myself and Mr Balfour, as well as be ready to do anything in your power for the young folk, I will give you five shillings above the three pounds.

There are just four of our young folk statedly at home, and we are often very quiet, though there is a hurry at a time. Any extra work that you may not be up to I promise to give you asistance in till you come into the way of it; but it will be a great comfort to me, as well as to yourself, if, when you have learned the method that I like, you endeavour to attend to it, not with eye-service, as a man pleases, but in singleness of your heart, as unto God.

Remember also that I admit of no gossiping. I give out the most of our washing, so I consider the work quite easy for two women when my rules as to method are attended to. I hope it is the next term that you intend to enter at, as the present kitchen servant leaves us at that time.

In spite of this rather daunting letter, Margaret went into service in Colinton manse.

In his children, and his grandchildren, the Revd Lewis Balfour inspired feelings of affection mixed with fear. R.L.S. remembered him thus:

A man of singular simplicity of nature; unemotional, and hating the display of what he felt; standing contented on the old ways; a lover of his life and innocent habits to the end. We children admired him: partly for his beautiful face and silver hair, for none more than children are concerned for beauty, and above all for beauty in the old; partly for the solemn light in which we beheld him once a week, the observed of all observers, in the pulpit. But his strictness

SWANSTON COTTAGE

and distance, the effect, I now fancy, of old age, slow blood, and settled habit, oppressed us with a kind of terror.

Nevertheless, the Stevenson family seemed to have been drawn to the Colinton area, for in 1867 Thomas, the father of R.L.S., leased Swanston Cottage up on the foothills of the Pentlands by Swanston farm, and kept the lease for 14 years. During the time he had the house, it became a haven for his son. As a young man, he used to stay there, often in wintertime, when he liked to shut himself off from the world and sit by the fire with his dog, dreaming his dreams. It was a place that fired the imagination. Built at the time of the so-called restoration of St Giles Cathedral, it had somehow acquired in its walls and in the garden some of the old gargoyles and crockets of the cathedral, and the youthful writer, no doubt influenced by these medieval relics, was to remember the house as having 'something of the air of a rambling infinitesimal cathedral'.

On one occasion, when R.L.S. walked down to the church, his visit made a vivid impression on one small boy, Alexander Fairgreave, whose father owned the nearby Kirkland Mill. Alexander sometimes used to go over to the graveyard from the mill and talk to the grave-digger. One afternoon a rather quaint fellow dressed in a long black coat and a sombrero-type hat wandered into the graveyard and came up to join them for a chat. After he had gone on his way, the child asked the grave-digger: 'Who was that?' –'That was the auld minister's daft loonie of a grandson, Robert Louis Stevenson,' he was told.

In the manse garden there was learned 'a kindness for the neighbourhood of graves, as homely things not without their poetry – or had I an ancestor a sexton?' wrote R.L.S. in *Memories and Portraits*.

In 1881, the year after his wedding in America, Robert Louis brought his wife Fanny to Scotland and they spent the summer in Pitlochry and Braemar. The following year, still searching for somewhere to live which alleviated the distress caused by his illness, he returned to the Highlands in the spring.

Perhaps on one of those visits he called upon Dr William Lockhart, his grandfather's successor at Colinton manse, and recaptured some of his childhood memories. Perhaps then he was invited into his grandfather's study where he had, 'quaking indeed with fear', repeated the psalm he had been required to learn, hoping against hope that if he said it well he might be rewarded with one of the Indian pictures on the wall which had been sent home from a foreign-based uncle.

Perhaps then, too, he had paused under the yew tree. 'Under the circuit of its wide, black branches, it was always dark and cool, and there was a green scurf over all the trunk among which glistened the round, bright drops of resin.'

And how was the deodar tree progressing, which had arrived as a seed in an envelope from his eldest uncle in India? At any rate, when the Stevenson family settled at Hyeres in the South of France a little later, R.L.S. worked on *A Child's Garden of Verses*, so many lines of which evoke the writer's childhood times of staying in Colinton manse.

> *Whenever Auntie moves around,*
> *Her dresses make a curious sound;*
> *They trail behind her up the floor,*
> *And trundle after through the door.*

R.L.S. particularly loved the Water of Leith, which flowed round the elbow of land that was the manse garden, and worked the nearby mills.

> *On goes the river,*
> *And out past the mill,*
> *Away down the valley*
> *Away down the hill.*

With his cousins he used to be tempted by a gap in the wall above the river tumbling by:

> *Over the borders, a sin without pardon,*
> *Breaking the branches and crawling below,*
> *Out through the breach in the wall of the garden*
> *Down by the banks of the river, we go.*

Here is the mill with the humming of thunder,
Here is the weir with the wonder of foam,
Here is the sluice with the race running under—
Marvellous places, though handy to home!

Sounds of the village grow stiller and stiller,
Stiller the note of the birds on the hill;
Dusty and dim are the eyes of the miller,
Deaf are his ears with the moil of the mill.

Years may go by, and the wheel in the river
Wheel as it wheels for us, children, today,
Wheel and keep roaring and foaming for ever
Long after all of the boys are away.

Home from the Indies, and home from the ocean
Heroes and soldiers we all shall come home;
Still we shall find the old mill-wheel in motion
Turning and churning that river to foam.

You with the bean that I gave when we quarrelled;
I with your marble of Saturday last,
Honoured and old and all gaily apparelled
Here we shall meet and remember the past.

The manse may have seemed to R.L.S. to be an unchanging symbol of the past, but in fact the building was altered many times over the years, and has continued to be. The Revd Norman Maclean, who was to occupy it in 1903, recorded its history as follows:

The generations have each left their mark on the old house. When in time the desire for greater comfort necessitated an enlargement, a large block with larger rooms was erected beside the small old house, and the front door moved westward, so near the rising ground that carriages had to go to the back door.

The phaeton bringing R.L.S. out from town to see his grandfather for the last time, had to draw up at the back door in what he later described as an 'unlordly fashion'.

Dr Maclean continued:

But with the next generation the manse was altered again; bow windows were struck out here and there, the door was shifted from the west to the east; and if driving up to the front door constitutes lordliness, then the old manse was on the way to it. Now more changes have been made in the old house, a new room has been added with a bow window overhanging the river, so that one can take a rod and cast a fly from it into the earthy, wheel-tossed water. In the days when the Water of Leith was a noisome sewer, no window could have been placed there; but in these days of its sweetness, the angler comes up trespassing under the panes.

In 1875, however, the church very nearly abandoned this historic old manse in favour of a new one to be built either on the glebe or at Craiglockhart. The principal reason given to the harassed heritors and landowners who had to give consideration to this major proposal was 'because of the nuisances that have sprung up around it'. Dr Lockhart, the incumbent at the time, made no secret of the fact that he did not like having noisy and smelly mills as neighbours. He had a supporter in the most active of the heritors, Mr R A Macfie of Dreghorn, but he did not favour Craiglockhart as a site at all.

Mr Macfie conducted a spirited campaign, even including a postal ballot to householders in the parish, against the Craiglockhart proposition. He wanted the new manse to be in the glebe, the piece of land on the other side of the road from the church, which would be 100 feet above the Water of Leith and more than 600 feet away from the nearest mill. Mr Richard Trotter of Morton Hall joined in the battle with a reasoned plea that neither site was suitable. In the end nothing was done, and the manse of R.L.S.'s fantasies remained. 'Out of my reminiscences of life in that dear place, all the morbid and painful elements have disappeared. That was my golden age ...,' he wrote.

The question of a new manse has rumbled on ever since – a full feasibility study was carried out in 1987, when it was even considered dividing the manse into two dwellings, and building two houses in its garden. However, when they were consulted, the incumbent family, the Johnstons, all declared firmly that they wished to remain in their historic old house, and the planning authorities did not look too enthusiastically upon any development plans for this List B building and Green Belt garden. Renovations were once again put in hand.

The suitability of the church fabric itself also came under question. The expansion of the parish had caused the establishment of an iron church at Craiglockhart in 1880. This modest building was subsequently moved, lock stock and barrel, to Juniper Green to accommodate the growing numbers of parishioners there, and it finally became the church hall in Dreghorn Loan, affectionately known as the 'Tin Hall'.

Earlier, in Dr Balfour's ministry, it had been decided that the church building was not large enough, and the architect David Bryce was asked to broaden the main seating area and put in new external stair-towers. The bell-tower at that time was at the back of the church, but its size displeased one of the parish residents, Lord Cockburn at Bonaly Tower, who, although he did not actually attend the parish church, evidently cared about its appearance. On 18th October 1837, he penned his opinions to Dr Balfour in a letter which is still in the church archives:

> *My dear Sir,*
> *It grieves me to think that our parish spire is likely to remain unraised. It is too low already; and the increased size of the church makes it still more paltry. It is really unworthy of the most beautiful site in the country. The heritors can't be expected to do more, <u>as heritors</u>; and it is plaguy to get at them in this character. But very little is required, and you have surely individual friends of the Church who will voluntarily give the mites that are wanted. I am told that £30 will raise it about twenty feet. Now I am confident that, if applied to, there are many who would at once raise it <u>at the least</u> that height. I need only name Dreghorn, Comiston, Redhall, Woodhall, Spylaw, Colinton, etc.. To begin*

the matter, I set myself down for £2.2s, or, if necessary, for £3.3s; and if only eight or ten others will do the same, we may in a month see the spire twenty-five or thirty feet above its present level, and no longer a reproach to the parish.

It would not be reasonable to expect that you should take more trouble than you have done already in getting the church improved. But I send this to you, because if you think the scheme pernicious or hopeless, it is perhaps needless to proceed further. But if you agree with me in thinking it both practicable and important, then the simplest way will be for you – who have many slaves – to send a sensible man round with the enclosed subscription paper; and if you choose to send this <u>hortatory</u> along with it, as your exposition, it will save all trouble except that of getting answers. I shall take care that the said sensible man is paid for his errands. But any other way that you think better, pray adopt. Only don't let us be disgraced.

Yours faithfully,
H. COCKBURN

Lord Cockburn was a powerful persuader, and he got his way. Indeed, when the church was rebuilt at the beginning of this century, his tower was taken down and re-erected at the front of the building in a much more prominent position, where to this day it is such a distinctive feature.

In the 1870s, however, Dr Lockhart was not only displeased with his manse, but with the church. Mr Macfie of Dreghorn once again leapt to the fore, this time with the radical suggestion that the church be moved out of the Dell altogether. He offered a piece of his own land at Dreghorn or at Redford for the new building.

On 22nd November 1877, Dr Lockhart wrote to him:

My dear Mr Macfie,
I have been much gratified with your handsome offer. Nothing would give me greater pleasure than to see a new Parish Church on some part of the Dreghorn lands; and if the hearty consent of Sir William Carmichael, Sir James Foulis and one or two others could be obtained, the thing would be done. I will wait however until

you communicate with these parties (for it would be better I think that you should do it) before calling any meeting .... '

But having built their church and manse in the Dell, the people of Colinton – and, it was suspected, the very influential laird of Colinton House – wanted them to remain there, and so they have. Dr Lockhart, whether he liked it or not, had to continue to robe in the manse, for then there was no vestry, and make his way through the tomb-stones to the church for services. On winter evenings he was met at the yew tree by the beadle carrying a lantern. Hapless late members of the congregation hurrying down the path would be startled by the spunky sight of a small pool of light bobbing among the graves and the shadows of black-robed figures. Even in the church the atmosphere was eerie. Tin lamps borrowed from the village were strung round the iron pillars that supported the gallery and the flickering light of candles threw long fingers from the front of the gallery. Small wonder the imagination of the child Robert Louis Stevenson had been so affected by this church.

R.L.S. was not the only famous man of letters to frequent the parish. Thirty years earlier the people of Colinton had become accustomed to seeing on the streets the elderly figure of Henry Mackenzie, that celebrated figure of the Scottish Enlightenment who, towards the end of his life, liked to spend the summer months in the tiny cottage in Bridge Road, near the traffic lights. Henry Mackenzie is commemorated there by the bald statement that he was author of *The Man of Feeling*, but in fact he did a great deal more than pen this sentimental novel, new genre though it was. He convened a committee enquiring into the authenticity of the poems of Ossian, and more importantly, in 1786, in the periodical *The Lounger,* which he edited, he was among the first to recognise the genius of a young Ayrshire man he called 'a heaven-taught ploughman' – Robert Burns.

HENRY MACKENZIE
(painting by Colvin Smith by courtesy of the Scottish National Portrait Gallery).

A couple of years later he read an 'Account of the German Theatre' to a meeting of the Royal Society of Edinburgh, praising especially the work of Schiller, thereby not only creating an interest in Scotland in German literature, but inspiring and encouraging another Scottish writer, Walter Scott. Scott recognised this when he dedicated *Waverley* to Mackenzie, calling him 'Our Scottish Addison'. In 1807 Byron was another young poet to be encouraged by Mackenzie. When Henry Mackenzie's own collected works came out, they filled eight volumes.

But Mackenzie was not only a literary man. He was Comptroller of Taxes for Scotland, and, in a different field, he was so moved by the sufferings caused by the Highland Clearances that he was a prime mover in the foundation of the Highland Society of Scotland, which to this day flourishes as The Royal Highland and Agricultural Society of Scotland and runs the Royal Highland Show. His influence was enormous; he was a giant of a man. However, when the Colinton people passed him, as he went for a walk in the direction of his beloved Pentlands, or down the Long Steps to the Dell, they saw a kindly old man who more and more was spending his final years writing prayers and hymns. It is interesting that although the name of Hailes for the parish had fallen into disuse many years before, Henry Mackenzie liked to write at the top of his letters 'Haills', and headed one of the last hymns he wrote with 'Hailes'.

Another well-known person to come to Colinton at that time for the summer was the exiled Bourbon King Charles X of France. When Charles X and his family left France after the Napoleonic wars, they were given refuge at the Palace of Holyroodhouse. This, with the abbey, was a royal foundation. By law he could not be pursued for his huge debts while living in it. At first, however, he was virtually a prisoner, only daring to go out on a Sunday when the law could not catch up with him. Later, when his affairs were less fraught, he rented Baberton House as a country retreat, and, while a sentry guarded the door, he and his royal grandchildren enjoyed the house and gardens. The children practised archery and played La Crosse. A ceiling in the house in what was to be known as 'The King's Room' was ornamented with *fleur-de-lis* in honour of the time of the king's occupation.

Ordinary folk were also choosing to come to the parish, finding it a desirable place to live, and this quiet migration brought a new look to the area. It heralded the beginning of the villa development. The railway, which came in 1874, brought yet more people, but long before that many new houses were built in the Spylaw Bank area and pleasant wide streets of neat villas began to spread out south of Woodhall Road.

Not all the inhabitants of these new houses went to the parish church. In 1843 the Church of Scotland was rent apart by that extraordinary act of defiance against the Establishment – the Disruption – a schism caused mainly by the still vexing question of Lay Patronage. So strongly did the protesters feel on the questions involved, they walked out of the General Assembly which was that year being held in St Andrew's Church, Edinburgh, and they tramped down the hill to Tanfield Hall to make history. Throughout Scotland they took with them 474 ministers, two fifths of the ministry, and nearly 4 per cent of the Church of Scotland communicants, and they formed the New Free Protesting Church.

Colinton's minister, Dr Balfour, like many of his predecessors in the manse on similar occasions, now found himself agonising on a Church constitutional issue. Should he leave? Should he remain?

The Session also argued. Dr Balfour remained, but two of his elders left him – Sir James Forrest of Comiston and Mr Adam Penman of Bonaly – and along with other Colinton residents went to the services for the Protestors which were held in the ballroom next to the Colinton Inn. After the ordination of their dissenting pastor, Dr Thorburn, the fledgling congregations of Currie and Colinton walked together to the mill-house of Kate's Mill for an ordination dinner, a crusading procession which must have caused quite a stir in the village. Momentous scenes were once again being played out at the trysting place of Colinton's history.

CHAPTER 11
Victorian Heyday

COLINTON, like all the villages surrounding Edinburgh, was profoundly affected by the huge industrial expansion that went hand-in-hand with Victorian ingenuity and prosperity. The first sign that something significant was going to happen to the village was the opening of negotiations with various land-owners regarding the purchase of land for a new railway line. There were protracted wrangles on the various deals, and they dragged on long after 1874 when the line was opened. It was not, for instance, until 1882 that the Fleming brothers at Upper Spylaw snuff-mill received money for 'loss of amenity'. Some of the settlements were reasonable, some not. All William Hill received for the piece of land he gardened at Millbank, Boag's Mill, was one pound.

From the start, the heritors of the parish church objected to the proposal to bring the railway to Colinton, ostensibly because they had responsibility for the minister's glebe, a small part of which was wanted for the railway station, but prompted also by concern for their own land. At a meeting in 1864, to which only one of the twelve heritors came, and two agents of the absentee landlords Sir James Liston Foulis of Woodhall and Sir William Gibson-Carmichael, their disapproval was registered in strong terms. They had various reasons for their stance: 'This short branch would, it is believed, do greater injury to the amenity of the residences and to the property of heritors .... The river would be further polluted by increased production of paper, encouraged by the arrival of the trains .... The residences of the heritors on the water would become unhealthy .... In such a narrow district the introduction of a large number of navvies might be productive of disorder and Breaches of the Peace and of immorality in the

COLINTON VILLAGE IN 1890.

villages to the great and lasting increase of the parish burdens ....'

To the heritors' chagrin, their concern for the morality of the villagers and for the well-being of their property was in vain.

With the land deals came the noise. The people who lived in Low Colinton, and the part of it known as Janesfield, began to hear through the long working hours of the day the hammering of steel rails being laid along a new track from Slateford. Bridges, too, were being built hurriedly over the Water of Leith – an unknown young engineer named William Arrol from Glasgow had offered to erect the ironwork quickly. On a clear day, from the higher parts of the parish, the Colinton people were later to be able to see one of William Arrol's rather larger bridges – his Forth Railway Bridge.

A big change was also brought to the shape of the village. There had to be access to the station, which was difficult from the old bridge, so the road trustees decided to build a new bridge across the Water of Leith, west of the village, leading into Gillespie Road, with an access road to the station. The bridge was finished in 1873, and the railway line went under its arches.

By the following summer a small station had been built on a platform below the bridge, and at the top of Jacob's Ladder there

COLINTON STATION, WITH MRS KERR'S CHICKEN RUN BEHIND THE BOOKING OFFICE.

was a cottage for the station master, Mr John Kerr. Perhaps not on the plans there was also a chicken run behind the booking office which provided eggs for Mrs Kerr. On 1st August 1874, without any ceremony, the new branch line loop to Balerno was opened. The railway train had come to Colinton.

Overnight, what had been a rural settlement for centuries, reached from town only on foot or by horse, became a dormitory village. Colinton was not yet a suburb – the area was not incorporated into the city of Edinburgh until 1920 – but it was now possible for business people, and even schoolchildren, to catch the 8.36 a.m. train, get into Princes Street Station at 8.50 a.m., do a day's work, and come home in time for the evening meal.

The stream of commuters in their business suits and bowler hats, or school uniforms, hurrying down Bridge Road or up Spylaw Street, to converge on the railway station in the morning, and in reverse in the evening, was to become a feature of village life. And of course the traffic was not only from Colinton; townspeople soon found they could enjoy a day on the hills by taking a train out to Colinton, or Balerno. The easy access by train even brought a new golf course to the area – to Torphin.

A history of the club states:

Travel to the course was mainly by train to Juniper Green station, followed by a twelve minute walk uphill to the clubhouse. This walk gave the younger and fitter members a considerable advantage, and they invariably were first off the tee. After complaints by those not so fit, it was arranged that, on the arrival of each train, names would be put in a ballot and drawn for order of play.

The golfers had clearly overcome the trepidation of earlier passengers when they first ventured on a train. Lord Cockburn, for instance, in 1850 when he went to Dumfries by train from Edinburgh, did not enjoy the journey at all.

On my way by rail from Bonaly to Dumfries, on Monday, 15th September, I was seized with what from its frequency seems to be an attack generated by railways, and reached Dumfries in great torture and great danger. I lay in the inn there twenty-three days before I could be brought back to Edinburgh, and never can forget the horror, or the mercies, of the visitation.

Previous journeys had not appalled him quite so much, however, for he must have been one of the first commuters to Glasgow. In 1842, when he was a circuit judge in Glasgow for two weeks, he decided he could not stand the thought of spending the Sunday there, preferring to get home to Bonaly Tower:

One of our days was a Sunday, a very serious thing in Glasgow. To avoid its horrors, Lord MacKenzie spent the day at Possil. But I rather think I fell upon a better scheme. Because the Court having risen at six on the Saturday evening, I got into the seven o'clock train and found myself here [Bonaly] *at tea and an egg, before ten.*

He then took the train back on Monday in time for court.

For all this new coming and going, more homes, of course, had to be built. There was not an immediate mushrooming of terraces, but there came the slow spreading of housing on Redford Road, Thorburn Road, Westgarth Avenue and Dreghorn Loan. The

COLINTON COTTAGE, PENTLAND AVENUE – THE FIRST HOUSE BUILT IN COLINTON BY ROBERT LORIMER. IT WAS FOR HIS AUNT, MISS GUTHRIE WRIGHT.

architect Rowand Anderson was to build his villas in Woodhall Road, and Spylaw Bank Road and Spylaw Park were to become peopled with flourishing families. Robert Lorimer now began his close association with Colinton, building firstly Colinton Cottage in Pentland Avenue for his aunt, Miss Guthrie Wright, then more fine houses in his own inimitable style like Acharra in Spylaw Avenue, Hartfell in Spylaw Park, and Huntly in Gillespie Road. His distinctive Rustic Cottages in Colinton Road did not come until the turn of the century.

The advent of the railway train to Colinton did little to change the privileged lives of the gentry in the older houses of the parish. They retained their carriages, fine horses and large staffs, and spent the winters in their town houses. In the spring they migrated to a still rural Colinton, accompanied by nannies, governesses, cooks and maids, and took up residence in their large mansions. There was much evidence of Victorian prosperity.

A branch of the Foulis family still owned Woodhall, and the owner of Dreghorn Castle and Redford House, Mr R A Macfie, had money to spare to indulge in his unusual interest, the collecting of parts of demolished buildings. Evidence of this is still very visible. The Covenanters' Monument, whose joined Ionic columns came from William Adam's Royal Infirmary when it was demolished in 1884, was erected in Redford Road by Mr Macfie, as was the building known as the Drummond Scrolls, with its extraordinarily intricate carving, at the gate of Redford

THE DRUMMOND SCROLLS

House. The Scrolls, which had been part of the decorative frontispiece of the Infirmary three storeys up, were named after Lord Provost George Drummond who founded the Infirmary. Mr Macfie made them into a stable block, but nowadays they are a modern home.

R A Macfie also made his mark in other ways. He entertained royalty at Dreghorn – exotic royalty. In 1881 the King of Hawaii, King Kalakaua, visited the castle, and in 1895 Mr Macfie's son played host to the king's niece, Princess Kaiulani. Both planted trees to celebrate their visit – when the Army moved back into Dreghorn Barracks in 1992, great efforts were made to try to locate them in order to protect them.

Mr Macfie's connection with the King of Hawaii was a commercial one; he had a major investment in a sugar plantation there, and he spared no expense on the welcome and comfort of his royal guest. He made a grand temporary entrance hall at the Castle, carpeted in red and decorated with flags. Over the two lodge gates which lead to the Castle arches were placed, made of evergreens and heather, displaying the message 'God save King Kalakaua', and the Hawaiian greeting of 'Aloha'. (The word 'Aloha' can still be seen carved on one of the chimneys of the lodge house in Oxgangs Road.) King Kalakaua must have amused Robert Louis Stevenson with tales of his visit to the writer's beloved Colinton, when they met in Hawaii in 1889.

Gracious living and entertainment – though not on quite such a grand scale – was also recounted across the valley at Hailes House, a fine mansion built in about 1765 and set in three acres of carefully designed gardens. The owners of the house at the turn of the century were the Craik family, and the mistress of the household, Gertrude Honora, enjoyed recording in her diaries the comings and goings of the large family.

She and her husband travelled a great deal – leaving the children with their nursemaid and governess. They went to Oberammergau in 1890, and on another holiday to Rome. After her visit to St Peter's she wrote:

I believe the presence and known desires of the Pope, orderly seats, and plenty of vergers about, would do a great deal to improve things, and (not least) the prohibition of spitting in the sacred buildings.

In the year of 1897, Gertrude Honora decided to keep a diary purely about the garden at Hailes, and in it she paints a picture of trips down south in search of plants and seeds, or forays into friends' gardens for cuttings, and long discussions with her gardeners about the flower beds.

They did things on a grand scale. From Naples they ordered five hundred white lily bulbs and two thousand narcissi. They had large greenhouses which were constantly in use for potting and forcing, a fernhouse which provided winter foliage to decorate the town house for dances and dinner parties, a tomato house, a fruithouse for storing apples and pears, and a vinery.

GERTRUDE HONORA CRAIK

With humour, gentleness and sometimes with a little pride, Gertrude Honora wrote about her garden. She particularly loved the huge holly hedges which divided the garden into three – these hedges had been much in fashion for a long time, for they were to be found at Colinton Castle, Dreghorn and Redford. Joseph Sabine, writing to the Horticultural Society of London in 1827, claimed that the Colinton hedges – originally 4500 hollies – had been planted as long ago as 1670 to 1680, 'certainly not later than the latter year'. In Gertrude Honora's time these had grown to about forty feet high, but they do not seem to have impressed her all that much. At Hailes House the hedges had archways cut in them to allow paths to run the whole length of the garden, and with careful pruning they had not gone straggly.

> *The hedges are a perfectly even wall of glossy green; no holes in them, such as I have often seen in rival hedges equally tall. Our hedges have been trimmed and cut with loving care and consequently show their gratitude with perfect symmetry.*

Apart from being a successful plantswoman, Gertrude Honora was also a keen photographer – one week the family had four cameras at work in the garden. Under one photograph she put the caption 'Old Stone above Garden Door'. The subject of her picture was the second century Roman carving of the Matres.

But as Gertrude Honora went about her innocent ploys at Hailes, half a mile away many of the people of Colinton had a very different way of life. Victorian prosperity did not bring much comfort to them. For instance, in 1886 half the population of the village of Slateford was wiped out by an epidemic of cholera, contracted, it was rumoured, from clothes brought to Inglis Green for bleaching, or from the rags used at Kate's Mill for processing into paper. The weeks that the disease raged had all the horrors of the plague. People fled, the shops closed, and the doctors had to turn the community hall into a hospital. Only the movements of those nursing the sick or attending to the dead were heard.

While Gertrude Honora's children were playing tennis, or going on pony-and-trap expeditions to Torduff, or quietly doing lessons in the Hailes schoolroom, there were children in the village who were working 13 hours a day in the mills. In spite of the ire of the School Board in the parish, truancy from the day school was frequent, not necessarily because the children did not want to go, but because they were needed in the fields or in the mills to help make ends meet. Apprenticeships for many of the crafts began in the early teens.

Conditions in some of the work-places were very unhealthy. The *Edinburgh Courant* in 1856, for instance, described the West Mill as 'an abominable, stinking place'. These mills gave employment to many of the Colinton people. Clad in coarse clothes and wearing clogs (an area of willow trees on the Woodhall Estate was especially grown for the manufacture of these clogs), a stream of people clattered down the roads and lanes leading to the mills early every morning for a long day's work.

The farms and the quarries also provided work for many, but domestic service gave a livelihood, of a sort, to the largest number. The ten large mansions employed cooks, table maids, kitchen maids, nursemaids, butlers, gardeners, coachmen and grooms.

These servants worked long hours, often in unpleasant below-stairs conditions, with little reward. The servants' hall was seldom endowed with many luxuries.

Other people in the village were carpenters, blacksmiths, shopkeepers, slaters, bakers and innkeepers. Worst off, however, were the agricultural labourers who were paid less in the winter than the summer, and who lived in tied cottages with little security, often merely a single room furnished with box beds. The 1881 census revealed that of the 746 inhabited houses in the parish, 253 had only one room and 306 had only two rooms. The exceptionally severe winter of 1895 may have been fun for the Currie curlers who were able to have a match on the dam-head of the Water of Leith, but there cannot have been much joy in the homes of the farm labourer at Swanston, or at Bonaly, who was on short-pay for winter, and who had no money to buy the fuel he needed so badly.

Jobs were never safe. Mills with their wooden buildings and inflammable materials lying around were particularly vulnerable to fire, and when they burnt down, as they frequently did, scores of people were suddenly out of work. In 1867 Boag's Mill was destroyed by fire, in 1885 the Slateford Mill went up, and in 1890 Kate's Mill had the same fate and seventy workers were out of work.

Mechanisation was also affecting employment. West Colinton Paper Mill, for instance, was converted to a steam-mill and many of the hundred employees were no longer needed. The same happened on the farms which acquired more efficient ploughs and threshing machines. In Hailes and Redhall quarries, too, jobs were not secure, for they depended upon the requirements of the builders in Edinburgh. After the New Town had been built, there was never again such a large market for stone from there.

When James Ballantyne described Colinton in 1844 in *The Miller of Deanhaugh*, he wrote 'with its romantic valley, its long rows of cottages embedded in the hollows, its shoals of rosy urchins, its myriads of white ducks, its kail yards, and their rows of currant bushes, its cheerful old matrons, with their close-eared caps, and its healthy old carls, with their broad blue bonnets, seated on door-stones sunning themselves'. He had clearly never glanced at the inscriptions on the stones in the crowded graveyard which paint an entirely different picture of life in Colinton. Nor did conditions improve much as the century went on.

Not surprisingly, with calamity never being far from the door, Friendly Societies had over the years sprung up in Scotland and there were some of these in the various communities of Colinton. With their arrival a chink began to appear in the forelock-touching reverence which had existed since feudal times between villager and landowner. The gentry may still have been flourishing, but when the new century came in, things were never going to be the same again.

Even in the ways of the parish church there were considerable changes. When Dr William Lockhart took up his ministry in Colinton in 1861, he was the first minister in the parish to be elected by popular vote, and in the *Imperial Gazetteer of Scotland* the patrons of the church were now described as 'the Communicants'. The long battle begun by the parishioners in 1783 when the patron, the Earl of Lauderdale, forced his protégé Dr John Walker upon them, was over. Complete abolition of lay patronage in Scotland came in 1874, and in 1895 parish councils were established to take over the functions previously carried out by the old parochial boards.

There were other churches in the parish, too – a Free church, an Episcopal church which also took the name of St Cuthbert's, and a United Presbyterian church at Slateford. There was a new spirit of tolerance, and all the Protestant churches in the parish were to encourage a scheme which got underway in 1889. That year the Aged Christian Friend Society of Scotland set up a fund to provide pensions for needy people, and then brought to Colinton one of the earliest sheltered housing complexes, designed primarily to help men and women who had spent most of their lives in tied houses and had nowhere to go when their employers turned them out.

There was plenty of scope for a concept like this in Colinton; so many of the people were still gardeners, domestic servants, farm labourers and quarrymen living in cottages which belonged to the big estates or companies. The Cottage Homes were not, however, only for Colinton people, and for a century now

The Colinton Cottage Homes, between Redford Road and Thorburn Road. The original cottage (centre) was built not far from the Sixpenny Tree..

men and women from all parts of Scotland have come to enjoy retirement in these neat little houses. A block of eight cottages on a site just off the Redford Road, near the Sixpenny Tree, formed the beginning of this enterprise; now there are 44, looked after by three wardens and a gardener.

The start of the new century was to see the end of the long ministry of Dr Lockhart. When he died in 1902, he left a parish in which there were now 5499 souls, which still depended very much on the Water of Leith for the milling which brought work, and which, in spite of the railway, was still largely rural. He had paid due respect in the pulpit on the death of Queen Victoria, and had said Godspeed to the young men who were marching away again to war, to fight 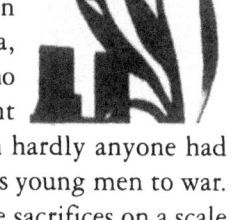 the Boers in places in South Africa which hardly anyone had heard of. But the village had always given its young men to war. The new century, however, was to see these sacrifices on a scale never before imagined, and for the first time, too, its women were to go on active service.

CHAPTER 12

The Village Suburb

WHEN the bells rang in the twentieth century, the parish of Colinton was still rural. Well over half of its area was arable land and nearly a quarter of it hill pasture. The sloping landscape was carpeted with fields spreading out in all directions, and cows and pigs were kept in backyards.

The landowners had laid out their grounds with care. A contemporary Agricultural Survey of Midlothian commended the plantings and 'the manner in which they are disposed, not in extended and thick plantations which turn a county into a forest and throw a gloom upon the prospect, but in clear and diversified lines, in clumps and hedgerows, useful as well as ornamental, protecting not injuring cultivation'.

Although the 1901 census gave the population of Colinton as 5499 souls living in 1005 houses, it was still largely a parish of mansions and cottages, with the new clusters of Victorian villas tending to sit primly along High Colinton and Low Colinton within easy reach of the railway. However, things were soon to change. Within 15 years, houses had spread up Dreghorn Loan, and the fields between Spylaw Bank House and Gillespie Road had become the trim gardens of rows of suburban homes.

People, though, were not only moving in to Colinton, they were moving out. The Balerno loop line was often the first stage of a long journey for families leaving the village, perhaps for ever, to seek their fortunes abroad. One such emigrant was James Milne, a well-kent person in the neighbourhood. In 1906 Canada beckoned him, and he worked for a time moving freight with ox-hauled carts on the Edmonton–Athabasca route. In due time he built himself a homestead and farmed; and when the

Canadian National Railways Company routed the railway line from Edmonton to Athabasca, it ran through his property. James Milne donated the land to the railway company for the building of the small railway station there, and in return he was invited to choose its name. He called it Colinton after his Scottish home.

Around this station grew the village of Colinton, Alberta, which still exists today, although the railway no longer brings passengers and the little station has been demolished. It has – like its namesake village, become a dormitory suburb, and its inhabitants work either in Athabasca or in the nearby oil and gas fields. In the First World War, however, such was the tug of patriotism that a son of James Milne crossed the Atlantic to join the armed forces of a land he hardly knew. He lost his life, and his death is recorded in the Kirk Session minutes of Colinton in Midlothian.

JAMES MILNE

Colinton, Alberta, was not however the first place to be named by a wandering son. John and Robert Balfour had in 1842 emigrated to Queensland, Australia, and had established a sheep and cattle station in the Brisbane Valley. Homesick perhaps for Colinton in Scotland, where they had grown up, they called their new home Colinton and the name remains to this day on Australian maps.

At the turn of the century in Colinton, Midlothian, there was yet again talk of building a new church to accommodate the fast-growing population in the parish. Already a church had been founded at the Craiglockhart edge of the parish. In 1880 an iron church had been established and this was replaced by a handsome stone building in 1890.

At Colinton Church the lack of space was not the only problem. The ventilation was totally inadequate and the musty smell was so pervading that it was believed that it came from the dead bodies buried centuries ago beneath the building. Some parishioners even refused to come to the church for fear of asphyxiation.

So when the Revd Norman Maclean succeeded Dr Lockhart, who had died in the parish in 1902, the controversy of the last century over sites and buildings was merely carried on. Mr Maclean belonged to the new church lobby. He wrote:

> *Colinton Church, crowded with pews, reeking with the atmosphere of a mortuary, devoid of every comfort, was one of the most primitive churches in Scotland. It did not even possess a vestry. It had no lamps nor lighting of any sort. When I preached before being elected, lamps were borrowed from the villagers, and candles, stuck in their own melted grease along the front of the gallery, illumined the shadows that darkened the corners.*
>
> *The 'band', as the folk in The Row called the choir, sat in the front two pews with their backs to the congregation. An ingenious jointed metal bracket, which was pulled out of the side of the pulpit, held a bowl of water in a casket when required for baptism. A wooden peg at the top of the pulpit stairs was provided for the preacher's silk hat. There was no Communion Table ....*

Enthusing to his Session Clerk one day about the architecture suitable for 'a real church', Norman Maclean said that he liked churches to be built after the form of a cross laid on the ground, with a nave, transepts and a chancel representing the head-rest of the Cross. His Session Clerk, Mr Andrew Shankie, was not, however, so keen. 'We have nothing idolatrous like that here in Colinton,' he interrupted.

The minister also wanted the new church to be built on a different site. The graveyard prevented suitable expansion of the old church. He had not, however, reckoned with the power of Colonel Trotter of Colinton House and his fellow heritors, most of whom did not wish the church to be removed from its hollow in the Dell and most of whom were also reluctant to finance the building of a new church, even on its present site. The controversy grew, and was aired in lengthy letters and reports in *The Scotsman*.

Thinking about the problem whilst walking up to Bonaly from Woodhall Road, Mr Maclean bumped into Mr J J Galletly, a newly admitted elder. This chance meeting proved to be momentous for the parish church, and Mr Maclean was fond of pointing out the exact spot on the road where history was written.

'The day of heritors is past,' Mr Galletly said crisply to Mr Maclean. 'Now what I would advise is that you call an early meeting of the Kirk Session, that we then resolve to rebuild the church, and if you care to appoint me Treasurer of the Building Fund, I will guarantee the Bank and we will start at once.'

Mr Galletly was as good as his word and the decision was taken to rebuild on the old site. Worship was moved to the church hall in Dreghorn Loan, and the demolition workers moved in. By 1907 Mr Maclean had his new (though not cruciform) church, designed by Sydney Mitchell. Parishioners were pleased to see the 1837 campanile rise from the builders' rubble in a new site over the porch, and an imaginative link with the past was maintained by the incorporation of the 1630 sundial of Sir James Foulis in the corner of the south wall.

The Scots millionaire Andrew Carnegie wrote from New York, promising half the price of a new organ, and a pulpit was presented to the church by Mrs George Balfour in memory of Dr Lewis Balfour, his son George, his grandson Robert Lewis Stevenson and his great grandson Lt Lewis Bradbury. Interestingly the Kirk Session minutes recording this fact stick strictly to the original spelling of 'Lewis' in the name of R.L.S..

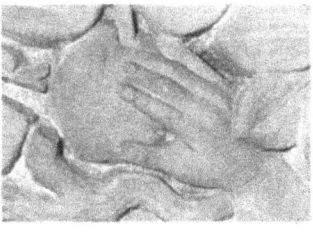

IN TODAY'S CHURCH, THE PILLAR ABOVE THE FONT IS CARVED WITH A HAND STRETCHING OUT TO PLUCK AN APPLE.

The new church was opened in April 1908 and in 1910 the Session showed its appreciation to Mr Galletly for his initiative by presenting him with an inscribed box made from one of the rafters of the 1771 church.

Encouraged by his success with the building, Norman Maclean attempted other bold things in his ministry, but he rarely found his efforts plain sailing. When he proposed to start a branch of the Woman's Guild, and had a Deaconess come to tell the women of the church all about it, the peaceful meeting was suddenly interrupted by a fusillade fired by one of the ladies of the parish.

'For my part,' she cried, 'I do not want any nuns disguised as the Woman's Guild spying about the parish. I am credibly informed that the new Guilds are merely disguised agents of the Jesuits, to bring us all again under the yoke of Rome. I don't want anything to do with anti-Christ and all his ways.'

Less contentious was Norman Maclean's foundation of the Colinton Literary and Debating Society – a society which continues to entertain the people of Colinton throughout the winter. One of its earliest debates resolved that it did not want 'the vulgarising influence of the tram cars to come any nearer', and one of the liveliest was a mock trial of a suffragist who had attempted to blow up Colinton Bridge. Many lecturers have talked of places far and near, but the most memorable in the society's history must surely be the night Sir Ernest Shackleton came to talk about his expeditions in the Antarctic.

No sooner had the controversy about the new church died down when an even more startling proposal shook the village to its very foundations. In 1905 news had seeped through from the lawyers' offices in town that negotiations were being carried on between the War Department and the trustees of Mr R A Macfie of Dreghorn, regarding the land lying between Firrhill and Redford Road, south of Colinton Road. The Army wanted the land to build Cavalry and Infantry Barracks. Colinton was appalled. By 1908 the Army's plans were public, meetings were held and the newspapers took up the story. The *Edinburgh Evening News* was scornful of the local opposition:

The proprietors and inhabitants of Colinton, to the number of sixty, on Saturday night held an indignation meeting against the proposal to plant down barracks in their vicinity. As much might be expected from property owners and snobs, who have a right to their opinions doubtless; but when in their hole-and-corner meeting they pass from opinions and deal with facts in an erroneous way, there is something to be said.

Take Sir Colin Macrae, who was shivering with fright owing to being faced with such a crisis as had never been known in the history of the locality. He has discovered that the proposed barracks would draw crowds of undesirables, cause great bustle and traffic, have a high wall round it, lead to the institution of public-houses, and the erection of great tenements. Where does he get his facts?

The Scotsman was only a little more restrained:

It is the invariable and inevitable effect of nearly all forms of city extension and the fulfilment of great public needs that they disturb the quiet and mar the beauty of the adjacent country. Even Colinton cannot expect to be exempt from this law of urban growth.

The Army won the day and not only built their barracks but, planning for the future, just five years later acquired, also from the Trustees of Mr R A Macfie, 'the lands, houses and other heritages' of Dreghorn for £35,000 'with the teinds parsonage and vicarage of the same lying in the Parish of Colinton and County of Edinburgh together with the seats in the Parish Church of Colinton effeiring to said lands .... '

The Redford Barracks were finished just in time to accommodate the soldiers training to go off to the First World War, but work on the Dreghorn Barracks had to be postponed until 1938. By the time the building was begun, the soldiers in the community had come to be regarded with respect and affection. Most of the able-bodied men in the village had themselves donned a service uniform and the people had watched all too often the poignant sight of the servicemen from Redford marching down to Colinton station to start their journey to the Front in France.

QUIETER TIMES IN THE VILLAGE STREET.

In the parish church it fell to Revd Thomas Marjoribanks to see the congregation through that cataclysmic time. Norman Maclean, a future Moderator, had moved to Glasgow in 1910. At the beginning of his ministry, Mr Marjoribanks, like his predecessor, tried to make some changes in the customs of the church – in the parish magazine made a quiet plea regarding marriages:

> *There seems reason to believe that the ancient and proper custom of celebrating marriages in Church is being revived in this Parish. During the present year two weddings have been solemnised in Colinton church, and both were of such a character as to show that there need be nothing ostentatious or elaborate about marriages celebrated in this way. There still exists in some minds the idea that the practice is a copying of 'English' ways. This is, however, far from being the case. According to the strict law of the Church of Scotland, no baptism or marriage should take place except in church. The <u>Directory for Public Worship</u>, our only authoritative guide in the matter, ordains as follows:*
>   *'Baptism is not to be administered in private places, or privately, but in the place of public worship, and in the face of the congregation, where the people may most conveniently see and hear.' And again, 'The minister is publicly to solemnize marriage in the place appointed by authority for public worship, before a competent number of credible witnesses, at some convenient hour of the day.' Let us hope that this return to the old paths will be a general one. Surely the House of God is a more suitable place in which to take the most solemn vows of a man's or woman's life than a crowded room.*

Dr Marjoribanks had an uphill struggle on his hands – baptisms and weddings were still recorded for some time in places like Hastie's Buildings, Colinton House Lodge and Inglis Green, but in the end he managed to get rid of the 'Englishness' of the concept of being married in church.

Sixty years on it was ruled in the Church of Scotland that 'the place, the hour, and the nature of the ceremony are not prescribed', but the present incumbent at Colinton, the Revd George Whyte, shares the same views as Thomas Marjoribanks:

After a couple of bad experiences conducting services in hotels, I have adopted a policy of only marrying people in church. As one old colleague said to me: 'You would not ask the surgeon to take your appendix out on the kitchen table.'

I am bound by the church not to refuse to marry people without good cause. Their desire to be married, say, on a mountain top seems good enough cause to me to refuse.

In the time of Dr Marjoribanks a new church room was opened above the manse 'offices', and the cracked church bell, which the minister said 'must have become painfully evident for some time to anyone with a musical ear', was recast. All building and renovations had to cease, however, after August 1914, and the parish magazine of September recorded that the minister had been conducting services on Sunday mornings at the camp for the force of Territorials who were in charge of the German prisoners. The prisoners themselves were being ministered to by a German pastor in Edinburgh.

The war effort, and the terrible sacrifices, now claimed the community. A 'For King and Country List' was carried in the parish magazines, listing all those serving in the armed forces. This was soon followed by a 'Killed in Action' list. The church hall was opened in the evenings for the Territorials, although the Session allowed no dancing.

The king's example of vowing abstinence from alcohol until the end of the war was supported by the Session – history does not relate how cheerfully – and working parties raised money, knitted garments, and collected fresh eggs for the wounded at the military hospital which had been established at Kingsknowe. On the fringe of the parish, the hydropathic at Craiglockhart had also been made into a military hospital. Among its patients who walked along Colinton Road to the village shops were the war poets Siegfried Sassoon and Wilfred Owen. In his room at Craiglockhart, Wilfred Owen wrote his 'Anthem for Doomed Youth', shortly before he went back to France to sacrifice his own doomed youth.

In 1917 the minister himself went to France, to work in the Scottish Churches' Huts, but he had returned to the pulpit by the time of the signing of the Armistice and he arranged the joyous ringing of the church bell and an informal service of thanksgiving and remembrance. Colinton, like every community, had paid a heavy price. Over one fifth of the men on the King and Country List never returned.

What was it like growing up in the manse during these tumultuous times? Sir James Marjoribanks, Dr Marjoribanks' son, who was born in the manse and went forth from Colinton to a career in the Diplomatic Service which was crowned by his appointment as Ambassador to the European Communities, looks back on his childhood in Colinton manse as fondly as R.L.S.. He was born in 1911, so he was too young to have these memories tinged by the tragedies of the First World War. Instead, he remembers going up to bed with his candle and enjoying, like the young Robert Louis, the satisfaction of coming 'from out the cold and gloom into my warm and cheerful room'.

Sir James's work took him all over the world, from Peking to New York, Bucharest to Canberra, but of the manse he claims:

> *I can never think of any house that bequeaths more of its graciousness and innate homeliness to its surroundings than this old gray mansion by the riverside, with woods rising to the sky all round it and yet with its lawns and flower beds always penetrable by whatever sunshine is going.*

His childhood games included climbing a ladder he and his brothers had made up the back of the yew tree trunk, and standing sixty feet up in the swaying branches 'with the smell of the yew berries and the sense of achievement at being on top of the world'. Then there was cricket on the manse lawn. 'Often the cricket ball would go through that breach in the wall of the garden [immortalised in *The Child's Garden of Verses*] and so to retrieve it down by the banks of the river we went. You were always "out" if you hit the ball into the Water of Leith (h.i.r. or hit in river). You were also "out", I hasten to say, if you hit the ball into the church-yard (h.i.c. or hit in church-yard).'

A Saturday ploy at the manse for Dr Marjoribanks and his eldest son, George, was to create a riverside walk right round the garden perimeter which was ceremoniously opened by the small daughter Anne, snipping an inaugural ribbon from her push-chair. On a Sunday the boys did a different job. Mrs Marjoribanks kept hens under the shadow of the churchyard and the Leghorn cockerel had a habit of crowing frequently – on Sundays as well as on other days. When it began in the middle of the sermon, Dr Marjoribanks, sensing there would be suppressed mirth in the manse pew and wanting to share the joke, was quite put off his stride, so in the end the boys' task before service was to catch it and lock it up in the stable.

Although closely in sympathy with R.L.S.'s reactions to the manse, Sir James takes exception to his statement that 'the old manse has changed today; it wears an altered face and shields a stranger race'.

> *I did not consider myself as part of a 'stranger race'. It was my lawn, my yew tree, my river just as much as R.L.S.'s. But in this thought lies perhaps the key to the garden's charm; it has been in a very personal way the perfect garden for a long succession of children.*

While the charm of the manse garden was untouched by the tragedy of the First World War, Colinton as a whole was greatly affected. In this watershed of history, even its separate entity went; two years after the end of the war, Colinton was swallowed up by the greedy boundaries of Edinburgh and the census no longer revealed Colinton's statistics. The landowning gentlemen began to disappear – the Dreghorn estate had already gone to the Army and the last of the Foulis family in the district, Sir Charles Liston Foulis, split up the estate of Woodhall in 1932 and sold it off to different parties. In 1926 the tramline was extended to Colinton. The nightmare envisaged in a Literary Society debate in 1903 had come true and Colinton had finally become a village suburb.

Shortly after this, the people of Colinton had another strange sight to behold. Bus-loads of boys in uniform shorts were

IN 1926 THE TRAMLINE WAS EXTENDED FROM CRAIGLOCKHART TO COLINTON AND ITS TERMINUS WAS AT THE FOOT OF WESTGARTH AVENUE.

deposited on the grounds of the Foulis estate at Colinton House, and their task was to pick up the stones on the fields. These were the boys from Merchiston Castle School, and they were helping to prepare the land for their new rugby pitches prior to the school moving out from the Napier Tower at Merchiston to Colinton.

For the local people the concept of a boys' boarding school established on English public school lines coming into their midst was a strange one. In fact, however, they found they were hardly aware of the school's existence. A Merchistonian who was in the group of boys picking up stones on the rugby field recalls: 'We had absolutely nothing to do with the village of Colinton. In three years at school there I cannot remember ever being in it.'

Behind the high hedges, enmeshed in their world of lessons, games, fagging, surnames, harsh discipline and unrelenting taboos, Merchiston boys came and went from Colinton leaving little impression on the community. Some of the local people may, however, have been amused at the incongruous sight of the prefects and those with games colours walking out of the school gates swaggering with walking sticks, as was their privilege, but still wearing their school shorts.

The ethos of the school is different now. Every week teams of boys go out to Colinton to do community service, mini-buses collect local residents to take them to school plays and concerts, and when the Queen came on the school's 150th anniversary, adults and schoolchildren of the village were invited to come into the grounds to see her arriving. Groups of boys – now in long trousers – regularly walk down to the village to get their cake and coke, and their blue tweed jackets are very much part of the village scene.

During the years after the First World War the pattern of life completely changed in Colinton. Fewer people lived and gained their livelihood in the community. There were not nearly so many farm jobs, residents did much of their shopping in town, and the mills ceased to flourish in such numbers. By the very nature of their construction and contents, the mills were very vulnerable to fire, and now they tended not to be replaced. In 1916 the great conflagration of Spylaw Mill, situated just beside the dominie's house, caused much excitement in the village, and it was never rebuilt. The grandson of the owner remembers the day of the fire well – as a small boy he heard the news while living in temporary accommodation in town because his house in Lauriston Place had received a direct hit from a Zeppelin bomb. The ruins of the mill remained in unsightly piles until 1921 when the land was finally cleared to make an extension to the graveyard. It was here that the war memorial was erected.

The passing years brought yet more expansion. Houses for the commuters filled up the green fields between the village and the Braid Burn, between Woodhall Road and West Carnethy Avenue, and ribboned along the boundaries of the garden of Hailes House. In the Wester Hailes area 17 small-holdings had been set up.

More parishioners meant more church accommodation was needed, and in 1925 a huge money-raising campaign was opened to find the funds to replace the old iron hall in the Loan which was sold for £65 to a firm in Leith. A piano was gifted for the new building and even dances were allowed – changed days indeed. A caretaker's house was built and there were yet more alterations inside the church. The organ and the choir were moved to the gallery, stained glass windows were put into the apse, and a committee was established to consider installing electric light.

The Colinton people were very concerned to preserve the amenities of their growing community – and in 1927 the Colinton Amenity Association was founded. This organisation has worked strenuously ever since to carry out its remit, suggesting environmental improvements, checking planning applications, monitoring traffic, guarding carefully the green spaces, and attending public enquiries.

In 1934 Dr Marjoribanks felt it was time to leave for a smaller parish, and it was Dr William Mackie Laing who was in the Colinton pulpit on 3rd September 1939, announcing to a shocked congregation that the country was once again at war. Shortly before the parishioners had come in, the troops from Redford Barracks had filed out early from their own service. The entry in the Chaplain's log book said simply:

> *9.30 parade.* *Sermon on 'Steadfastness' Eph. VI 13*
> *Remarks: Very wet. No collection taken.*
> *War Declared on Germany*

After October 1st no further parade services were held in 1939, though there was voluntary attendance by the troops.

For many of the Colinton people the routine of war-work was all too familiar. For some it spelt the end of a way of life; 'At Home' cards were put aside, tennis-party invitations abandoned, and winter dance plans cancelled, never to be renewed. Everyone set to, helping with the evacuation of the Colinton children, forming work parties to knit for the troops, and volunteering to help in the canteen set up by the parish church and the Episcopal church in the Loan Hall. In 1941, 87,952 meals were served to the men from the barracks, and the average number of cups of tea or coffee in a week was 3000. Even the schoolchildren helped. There were concert parties once a week, dances, a library, a mending party, billiards, table-tennis, and – thanks to new army boots and the parade ground – a constant queue for the chiropodists.

At the church the windows were protected against air-raids, an elder was appointed to remain at the outer door of the church during services to give warning of the air-raid siren,

A PRESS PHOTOGRAPHER RECORDS HISTORY REPEATING ITSELF – SOLDIERS MARCH ONCE AGAIN OVER THE TRYSTING PLACE OF ALL COLINTON HISTORY.

fire-watching teams of householders near the church formed a duty roster, and all evening meetings and the evening service were abandoned. An air-raid shelter was built in the garden of the caretaker's house. The 'Killed in Action' records began again, and for the first time women were on the 'For King and Country Roll'.

The local shopkeepers, teachers, accountants, students and mechanics all went into uniform too, in the Local Defence Volunteers which were to become the Home Guard. Many of them did their jobs by day and guarded the village by night. On duty in Spylaw House, which was then a youth hostel, on the night of 25th/26th June 1940, William Dobson wrote in his report sheet:

An Air Raid Warning was heard by 1st Patrol at 12.03 a.m. Patrol stated they heard sound of bombs bursting in the distance in the direction of Forth, and saw the bright flash of the explosions in the Grangemouth or Donibristle direction.

Cadet H. Snow, Varsity O.T.C., reported at this post at 12.30 a.m.

The 2nd Patrol saw two enemy aircraft caught in the searchlights, the first about due west of Bonaly, and the second passing over Corstorphine going in an easterly direction. Both machines were subjected to heavy anti-aircraft fire and were attacked by our fighters. The flash and explosion of bombs were heard at 1 a.m. west of Bonaly and at 2 a.m. apparently near Turnhouse.

All Clear sounded at 2.18 a.m.

Arms, ammunition and clothing were returned by patrols, checked, found correct and in good condition (11 armlets, khaki only.) The Post was left clean and tidy. Patrol dismissed at 7 a.m.

Safely away from this danger were many of the children of Colinton. Their parents, fearing the proximity of the barracks as targets for German bombs, sent them off on the special evacuation train to East Calder. Memories of this are still vivid:

In the summer of 1939 components of Anderson shelters were delivered to households and lay in the back gardens for months to provide an additional play-site for us children. Feverish assembly of these shelters and the digging of holes accompanied the declaration of war but we missed that as we had been evacuated on the 1st September. We assembled, most of us accompanied by tearful mums, at the local school and, after list checks and name labelling, were marched down to the station, where a special train was standing at the ready.

Although billeted with a Roman Catholic family, we went to church on the Sunday morning and heard the grave news that war had been declared; I can still recall the sombre threatening mood that hung over the congregation in that little historic church. We were there for one term and returned home in time for Christmas. On one Saturday my sisters borrowed bicycles and went for a run; pedalling up towards the Pentlands on the horizon, they suddenly realised they were on roads they recognised and so they continued home for a visit to a very surprised mother. After all, we were only some twelve miles west of Edinburgh.

Colinton Parish Magazine
DECEMBER 1941

SEARCHLIGHTS SWEEPING THE SKY TO PIN-POINT ENEMY AIRCRAFT DECORATED THE CHRISTMAS IMAGE OF THE CHURCH FOR THE 1941 PARISH MAGAZINE.

When the final Home Guard patrol had stood down and the war was over, there was of course another appeal for a suitable war memorial, this time for the 34 men who had given their lives. Apart from an inscribed memorial tablet to be put on the First World War stone in the cemetery, there was an imaginative scheme to have, if funds permitted, a Garden of Remembrance. This was to be in the grounds of Merchiston Castle School opposite the Rustic Cottages and overlooking the Dell, the church, and the war memorial.

The Governors of the school readily agreed to lease the ground for this purpose at a purely nominal rent. A Memorial Gateway was to be erected at the entrance on Colinton Road, and the development of the garden was to be progressive and commensurate with the funds available. The two schemes were estimated to cost £2500 but, for one reason or another, Colinton never got its Garden of Remembrance. Was the required money never raised?

The fallen in both wars were, however, to be remembered in a memorial within the church, a sculpture of the risen Christ by

Thomas Whalen placed in the alcove behind the font. At the same time there were considerable discussions about the cross-beam in front of the apse. The Session felt 'that the beauty of the apse would be enhanced by the removal of the cross-beam'. Expert opinion was sought. The matter was shelved, but raised again in 1969, when Mr George Keith was appointed by the Church's Committee on Artistic Questions to examine the structure of the apse. He reported that the removal of the apse beam would be possible, but would entail major work of demolition and construction. Once again the matter was shelved, but it reared itself again in 1992 when the 900th Anniversary celebrations were being discussed.

Just as the First World War had precipitated the vote for women, so did the Second World War advance the cause of sex equality. But it took time. Not long after the memorial service held on Victory-in-Europe Day, there came a request from the Presbytery of Edinburgh for the opinion of the Kirk Session and the congregation on the question of admission of women to the Eldership of the Church. By eight votes to seven, the Session agreed to admit women, but the congregation was strongly against the idea. When the vote was counted, only 60 were for, 109 were against, and 30 were neutral. It was to be another 22 years before the first two women were admitted to the Eldership in Colinton, and even then there was considerable concern. Many people in Colinton still did not like the old order to be changed.

CHAPTER 13
The Hills of Home

THE old order in the parish church saw a radical change in 1964 with the retirement of Dr Laing and the appointment as minister of the Revd William B Johnston. For a start, he almost immediately became known throughout the parish as Bill, even in his Moderatorial year, yet this familiarity never bred disrespect. Among his parishioners he was quickly esteemed for his logical, scholarly and often topical sermons, and his bottomless reservoir of patience and tact.

'It may have taken all night, but Bill could get the most controversial decision through the Session without upsetting anyone,' was the comment of one elder.

Bill Johnston also moved with the times. The question of women in the Eldership came up again. On 13th February 1967, the Kirk Session minutes record:

> *The Kirk Session had before it certain nominations from members of the congregation together with the Session's own suggested names. As among the nominations the names of women appeared, the Kirk Session first discussed the desirability of their being included in their considerations.*
>
> *On a vote being taken, following a very full discussion, the Motion was carried by a majority ....*

After what was clearly one of Bill's late night meetings, this historic decision brought to the Eldership Mrs Isobel Smith and Miss Jenny Neilson. But for a long time the women were not listed alphabetically with the men on the elders' rotas, nor were they put at the beginning; their station in life was firmly at the end.

Miss Jenny Neilson was fairly awed by the prospect:

Both Isobel Smith and I realised that this innovation could be viewed by many as an experiment on which the future of women in the Colinton Eldership might depend, and the two of us spent many hours considering together the role and responsibilities of elders in general, and whether we, as women, while in partnership with the men, had any specific contribution to make to the life and work of the congregation.

We did not, however, feel that these questions were foremost in the minds of many of the congregation. 'But <u>what</u> will you <u>wear</u>?' was the question which arose time and time again, leaving us feeling that even our most sombre clothes (navy for one of us and dark grey for the other) could not possibly compete in dignity with the morning coats worn by our male colleagues.

Other members were engaged in questioning how we should be described — would the term '<u>lady</u> elders' or '<u>women</u> elders' be more appropriate? However '<u>women</u> elders' was the term accepted as being more biblical than the alternative, and so, I think, it has remained. We were however careful, at that time, not to sit together at Session Meetings, lest we appeared in any way separate from the '<u>men</u> elders'.

Curious aspects of the arrival of the women elders bothered the Session. What if one of them was unable to come to Communion? The symmetry of the processions up the aisles would then be distorted, and that would never do.

This danger was seen to be so great that at an early stage it was seriously suggested that perhaps we should not take part in these services at all, but a compromise was eventually reached in which, initially, we took part only in afternoon services, giving time for adjustments to be made to arrangements if either of us became unwell in the morning.

When it came to work in the Church Room kitchen, the men elders expected the women elders to do the washing up. This, they thought, was women's work.

It possibly caused some dismay when we made it quite clear that we would only undertake exactly the same tea-making, washing up and other domestic duties as were undertaken by the men.

The women elders felt the same about having a district. At first some of the men thought they should not 'be burdened' with a district, but time and Bill Johnston soon altered that.

The minister did not stop at that. The parish had got used to student assistants, some of them breezy Americans from the Fuller Theological Seminary in California sent by their expatriate Scottish preaching professor, Ian Pitt-Watson, to learn from the preaching expertise of Bill Johnston. On 15th December 1986, however, there is a brief statement in the Kirk Session minutes concerning a Scottish Assistant: 'The Moderator reported that the Assistant Minister for 1987/88 would be Miss Marion Dodd. She would commence her duties on 1st July.' If there was any all-night discussion on this radical move for Colinton it was not recorded, but the fact that on 14th December 1987 Marion Dodd was invited to remain another year as assistant speaks for itself. Colinton had accepted women ministers.

THE REVD MARION DODD

Marion Dodd was nervous of being Colinton's first woman minister:

Thoughts of working with Dr Johnston were daunting, to say the least. His reputation in the pulpit and in the courts of the Church was such that I feared I could never match up. However, on my first meeting in his study, I discovered a lovely man, wise but compassionate, and with a lovely sense of humour. It was months later that I learned of his grave scepticism at the thought of a lady in his pulpit.

On the principle that in Colinton things were never done by halves, Bill then proceeded to show his approval of women ministers by appointing another to join the team. Thus arrived a young Californian, the Revd Libby Carlson, who frequently began her day by jogging round the parish in shorts.

Libby – she was never known as anything else – was surprised to find the parishioners all having a slight sense of schizophrenia.

> *The people outside the church are really different than when they come inside. It's a weird transition, but you can be with them outside and they're chit-chatting and making jokes, and then they seem to come in the door and their whole countenance changes. They get very serious and very dour and sombre – not looking up at you even, and you think 'Who are these people? I don't know them'. I attribute the seriousness with which they take religion to the Knoxian times.*

Things changed. One Sunday, Libby told the children she had forgotten her breakfast, and she sat, in her gown and hood, on the chancel steps and poured cornflakes and milk into a bowl and proceeded to eat them, the crackling of the cereal reaching the back pews over the microphone. The children were enchanted, but at the same time Libby produced a message out of all this which was apt.

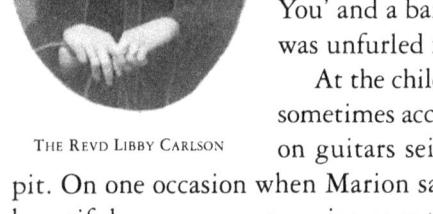

THE REVD LIBBY CARLSON

The women assistants were not only unceremonious with the children. At Christmas they put a Santa Claus hat on Bill Johnston's head, and on his birthday the children sang 'Happy Birthday to You' and a banner of birthday greetings was unfurled from the choir balcony.

At the children's address the story was sometimes accompanied by music played on guitars seized from behind the pulpit. On one occasion when Marion sang to the children in her beautiful mezzo soprano voice, spontaneous clapping burst out from the pews. Indeed clapping and laughter now became quite natural and none was louder than when Bill Johnston in the pulpit pointed out the smart new notice affixed by the City of Edinburgh District Council on to the wall of the graveyard at the church gate which said: 'Improving Services, Creating Jobs'.

The services had therefore become much more informal. Elders were no longer required to wear morning dress for Communion, and the children found they had a large role to play in church. Would this have happened at that time if the assistants had been men? The mood was such that it probably would, but nevertheless the team of Bill Johnston, Marion Dodd and Libby Carlson had something remarkable about it.

Bill Johnston explained it this way: 'Well, the chemistry was different, and what I discovered was that women can do things in church that men would not attempt, and people will say things to women that they will not say to men. And they were two exceptional women.'

Over the years there were other changes. Individual Communion cups were introduced; the parish magazine was revamped with a new layout and glossy paper. An Easter Breakfast was started in the Loan Hall, and invitations to Communion replaced the returnable communion cards. The manse even got central heating – albeit only partial.

Bill Johnston was very alive to the social changes in Colinton. When he had come to the parish there was a large percentage of retired people living in the area. Now, with the new housing developments and the commuter way of life, the parish roll numbered many first-time house buyers with young families who would stay for a spell then move to a larger house elsewhere. Colinton had more baptisms than any other church in the Presbytery.

To cope with this influx of young children, Bill Johnston started the crêche in the newly furbished Yew Tree Room, and when Marion Dodd came along she had his support to found the Yew Tree Mums group, which gave an opportunity to young mothers and their toddlers to meet twice a week in the Session Room. Out of this grew the Yew Tree Pot Pourri, a meeting point for Yew Tree Mums in the evening, which later changed its name to the Colinton Ladies. Both these organisations were set up for the parish as a whole – in other words they were made open to people who were not actually members of the church.

Other age groups were catered for. Bill Johnston encouraged one of his American assistants, Talbot Svendsen, to establish his

MOVE! group for 16 year olds and upwards. Here, on a Sunday night, there were no subjects barred.

Meeting in the Yew Tree Room, they discussed unemployment, drug abuse, contraception, alcoholism and the ever worrying problem of AIDS. They did practical things as well, like going to Dundee to help to clean up and paint Whitfield Parish Church; and when Marion Dodd and Libby Carlson were in charge they took the MOVE! group, together with contingents from South Queensferry Parish Church and St Mark's Roman Catholic Church, to Northern Ireland to visit the Peace People Farm Project.

It was Libby Carlson who started the group for 14–15 year olds named FLASH, which had a programme similar to MOVE!, spiced with Saturday night visits to the cinema, pizzas and videos in the Loan Hall and 'Look in – Sleep Overs' in the Yew Tree room – with permission from the Session. FLASH adopted a child from Malawi, Grace Ndomomdo, for whose education they helped to pay. In 1985 the younger children of the Junior Sunday School chose the improbable name of JAWS for their own group – it stands for Junior Activities and Worship on Sundays – and Dr Johnston encouraged them to take part in services, with mime, acting and music. In 1991, Terry and Jan Chapman, also from America, founded a Young Couples Group.

It was not only the young who were coming into the community. At this time a large sheltered housing complex, Old Farm Court, was established on the site of the old farm of the Redford Estate, and another at Woodthorpe on Redford Road. Dr Johnston reacted to the needs of these incoming older residents as quickly as he did to those of the young, and not only were regular visiting arrangements made, but a rota of volunteer elders drawn up for driving the older residents in the parish to church. Colinton Community Care, an all-parish organisation, has also done a great deal to relieve the problems of the sick, the elderly and others in need in the neighbourhood.

Bill Johnston was not only busy at home. During the years since the beginning of his ministry at Colinton, his reputation grew internationally. He was always a keen supporter of the ecumenical movement, active on many Church committees and a member of the World Council of Churches. All this was recognised in 1980 when he was made Moderator of the General Assembly of the Church of Scotland, the fourth Colinton minister to hold this office. This meant that he was absent from the parish for a year, and another much-loved team – 'the reign of the three Georges', as Bill Johnston liked to call it – took over. The Georges all lived in the parish and they were the Very Revd Dr George Reid, the Revd George Lugton and the Revd George Monro. There must be something that attracts Georges to the parish of Colinton; when Bill Johnston retired, the locum-minister was the Revd George Elliot and the present minister is now the Revd George Whyte.

All was not, however, plain sailing, either then or later. For instance, when the Pope made his historic visit to Edinburgh in 1982 the Kirk Session minutes reveal that some members of the congregation had great anxiety about whether there were plans for the Church of Scotland to talk with the Church of Rome on the question of unity. Dr Johnston confirmed to the Session that no such talks were contemplated. The Pope was making a pastoral visit to members of his Church, and the General Assembly of the Church of Scotland had decided that it would be appropriate that the Moderator should meet him when he visited Scotland. The Pope was not visiting the Church of Scotland, Dr Johnston emphasised, but was having a personal meeting with the Moderator as the representative leader of the national Church. The anxieties were dispelled. Indeed, the congregation welcomed a Roman Catholic to preach in an ecumenical broadcast service.

Far greater anxiety seemed to be felt about the ever-present problem of the church – lack of cash. The Loan Hall needed to be renovated. Was Doohill, the house opposite the church, which had originally been bought in 1960 for extra space for meetings, Sunday School activities and possible accommodation for the church officer, now working its passage? A great fund-raising campaign was put underway to renovate the hall, and Doohill was sold.

Amidst these domestic problems there came the national crisis of the Falklands War, and Colinton was not untouched by

In 1983 the Queen was much amused when she visited Colinton on the occasion of the 150th anniversary of Merchiston Castle School
(*by courtesy of The Scotsman Publications Ltd*).

it. Colinton had been a garrison village since the First World War, and the movement of troops was of significance. Would the men at Redford have to go? The churchyard claimed a victim, but not from the barracks. The great-great-grandson of Dr Lewis Balfour was killed in action on the *Sheffield* and buried at sea, but the family recorded his death in the Balfour Tomb in the graveyard.

On the home front, the perennial problem of whether the manse should be kept was raised again. This time the minister and his family were totally opposed to any move, and when the Kirk Session produced a very business-like review of the whole question they sent a letter of reassurance to Dr Johnston saying that 'every effort would be made to enable you to continue to reside in the manse for so long as you remain our Minister, which we hope will be for many years to come'.

When the review was published, it was revolutionary. The Manse Review Committee had explored the possibility of dividing the manse into two, and of building two houses in the grounds. The Edinburgh District Council's reaction was far from enthusiastic. The manse was B Listed and could only be sub-divided if the internal and external character were not materially affected. The land surrounding it was in the Green Belt, and in addition was important to the character of the Listed group of buildings within the Colinton Conservation Area.

In the end the Session voted to retain the manse and somehow the money was raised to meet its huge repair bills and it was saved. Presumably the manse saga will go on and on, generation after generation, part of Colinton's rich tradition. The story of the Cemetery Bothy, however, finally ended in 1990 when the historic little building, which had been the dominie's house, was spared the indignity of being demolished to make way for a car park. Refurbished in a joint venture with the Cockburn Conservation Trust, it was sold to become a home.

The other premises of the church were being used to capacity. In the winter of 1990, use was made of the church halls by 52 organisations or groups, some of them church affiliated, some of them not. The Colinton Amenity Association, Literary Society, Colinton Local History Society, Garden Club, Cubs, badminton, dancing, blood transfusion services – the list of those who enjoy the amenity provided by this accommodation is long. While the church secretary is tapping away on her word processor in the

IN 1990 THE DOMINIE'S HOUSE, LATER THE CEMETERY BOTHY, WAS REFURBISHED IN A JOINT VENTURE WITH THE COCKBURN CONSERVATION TRUST.

LOCAL CHILDREN WATCH THE MARCH-IN OF THE 2ND BATTALION, THE SCOTS GUARDS, TO THE REFURBISHED DREGHORN BARRACKS, 1992.

church office, the keep-fit class is thumping away through the wall.

In 1991 the soldiers at Redford prepared once again for war: this time in the Gulf. It fell to Revd Terry Chapman from America, one of the assistants, to preach that fateful Sunday when hostilities were announced – Dr Johnston had become ill. Terry, who sometimes liked to talk in football parables, had no jokes in his sermon that day: 'What madness drives humankind to such extremes?' he asked. 'Do all these people have to die? Can we ever live in peace? Why can't love reign in our hearts?'

When the King's Own Scottish Borderers left Redford for the Gulf, the Session Clerk wrote to them sending the good wishes of the parish church.

Dr Johnston returned in the summer, but only for a brief spell until his retirement. It was almost a case of 'standing room only' at his Valedictory Service, and lunch was served for all that huge congregation in the Loan Hall. A similar event was held on the evening of 8th April 1992, after the Induction of the new minister, the Revd George Whyte. A bus brought some fifty members from Langside, Glasgow, to bid farewell to 'their' minister, and they took back with them memories not only of a moving service but of complete traffic chaos in the village when the whole congregation spilled out of the church and set off up the hill to the Loan Hall.

What type of parish had the new minister come to? Although over the last fifty years its population had increased, its boundaries had contracted. Colinton Mains had acquired its own church, albeit firstly a hut, in 1939, Oxgangs in 1957 and Wester Hailes in 1969, the last church, a transported union of several town churches, taking the name of Holy Trinity. This comes from its Medieval foundation church of Soutra, but, interestingly, it is the same name as that chosen exactly nine hundred years ago by Queen Margaret, mother of the founder of Hailes parish, for her church at Dunfermline. In 1992 the roll at Colinton Parish Church was listed as 1556 members.

The developers had also moved into the parish. In 1955 the children lost their sledging hill on Campbell's Field when it was cleared of scrub and 162 houses were built on streets named Redford Loan, Redford Avenue, Redford Terrace. More houses ribboned out of Woodhall Road, and at Bonaly the fields were swallowed up by a huge development which began in 1959 with Bonaly Terrace and Crescent and now amounts to over 500 homes.

In the 1980s, 24 houses and a new street name, Broomy-knowe, appeared on what had been a corner of the grounds of Merchiston Castle School, and at Woodfield Park sixty houses were constructed. On the paddock belonging to the Army opposite Dreghorn Barracks, the Gallolee estate of over ninety homes mushroomed.

Naturally over the years there were some casualties in the building developments. In 1955 Dreghorn Castle, which had seen so much history, was, after a spell of being a boys' prep. school, allowed to fall into disrepair and finally unceremoniously burned and bombed by the Army as a T.A. exercise.

THE 1980s COURTYARD DEVELOPMENT AT BONALY, ADJOINING EARLIER 1959 HOUSING ESTATES.

By the end of the 1980s most of the parish's manor houses had ceased to be gentlemen's country seats. Colinton House was the science block of a school, Redhall House was in the Graysmill School complex, Hailes House was an office, and Redford House, Spylaw House and Bonaly Tower were sub-divided into several homes. Woodhall House had a wing tacked on to it for a seminary for Jesuit priests.

Later, West Colinton House came down to make room for modern dwellings, and Woodfield House, previously occupied by the nuns of the Convent of the Good Shepherd, was demolished, again for a development. (Before the bulldozers moved in, the Edinburgh District Council, anxious that the chapel should be retained for religious or community use, approached the Kirk Session to see if the parish church could take it over, but the Session decided they could not possibly buy it.)

The huge influx of people into the new housing estates brought to Colinton the reign of the bus and the motor car, which now threatens to strangle it. The passenger trains had stopped during the Second World War; then in 1955 the trams were withdrawn and buses took over their routes. Business people and children used motor transport to get to town and school, and the roar of the lorries and cars thundering through the village made it almost impossible to speak in the shops. A new phrase crept into people's talk: 'When we get the Ring Route .... '

In 1960 it was estimated that 2500 vehicles a day would use a by-pass round Colinton. After many years a decision was finally taken to build the road, and in 1979 the Colinton section of the by-pass was begun. It was finished in May 1981 at a cost of twelve million pounds. Today more than 40,000 vehicles a day use it, and a new noise disturbs all the gardens of the southern fringe of the parish – the constant roar of traffic.

By the 1960s the schooling accommodation could no longer cope with the ever burgeoning numbers of children in the parish. In 1968 Firrhill High School, which serves Colinton, had to be extended, and at the same time an annexe was built in Redford Place to house the overflow of children at Colinton Primary School in Thorburn Road. By 1976 it was found that this was not enough and a new school at Bonaly Grove, Bonaly Primary School, was opened for 262 children. Colinton School, which now operates solely at Redford Place, has 40 nursery places and 160 pupils, 75 per cent of whom have fathers who are in the army or working for the Ministry of Defence, and it is the turn of Bonaly School to be bursting at the seams. With a roll of 450 children in the school and the nursery, it has had to press into service the old school building in Thorburn Road as an annexe, and it sometimes has a waiting list for pupils.

As the demography of the community has changed, so have the concepts of worship. Upon the platform of the innovative services and groups of Bill Johnston's ministry, the Revd George Whyte has built yet more flexible ways for parishioners to praise God and serve the community. The Sunday at Eight Service in the Loan Hall, begun principally because it had become unsafe for worshippers to go down to the Dell to church in the dark evenings, has been replaced by First Sunday, a series of broad-based meeting points at 5–7 p.m. when there is a choice of activities and the social enjoyment of a basket tea. A Holiday Club for children has been organised in the Loan Hall, and words like SWOT analysis, tasks and targets appear in the Kirk Session minutes.

There is also All Age Worship and Learning, an informal 9.30 a.m. service without a sermon, where the congregation break up into small groups to talk round the day's theme, while the children go to their classes in the Yew Tree and Session rooms. George Whyte has brought new hymns and songs to the services,

THREE-QUARTERS OF COLINTON PRIMARY SCHOOL CHILDREN
HAVE FATHERS IN THE ARMY OR WORKING FOR THE MINISTRY OF DEFENCE.

To cope with the burgeoning population,
a new Primary School at Bonaly Grove was opened in 1976.

and Palm Sunday is celebrated with the music of the church's own orchestra. Even more revolutionary has been the invitation to baptised children in the church to take Communion. Backed by a General Assembly resolution, the minister, so keen to involve the children in worship, has introduced this concept with great enthusiasm. One small boy was less impressed: 'When do we get the juice?' he asked his mother. 'Now,' she replied, as the individual glasses were passed along the pew. 'What?' he whispered. 'Is that *all* we get?'

Out in the parish George Whyte has found a community in love with the setting of the area. There is an old saw which says that when people are asked where ideally they want to spend their days, they will reply: 'Near water and trees, with open spaces, but not too far from other people.' This is Colinton.

The residents extol its leafiness, its hills and the river. They like its sense of community and its feeling of history, its proximity to theatres and galleries in the town, and its architecture. They are nostalgic about the shops that have gone – the village used to boast three grocers, two butchers, two sweet shops, two chemists and two newsagents, but they still allow an extra half an hour for 'chatting time' when they go shopping in the village.

The people of Colinton are not, however, totally uncritical. Some feel it is too parochial, some feel they can only make friends with other incomers, and some feel that only membership of one of the two churches provides the key to acceptance. The young tend to find it snobbish, and claim that there is not much to do at the weekends. There is also regret that the effects of Edinburgh's education system, with its proliferation of independent schools, lead to a divisiveness among neighbours and friends. It is possible to find in one street in Colinton the children in six neighbouring houses going to five different secondary schools – but this phenomenon is not peculiar to this parish.

The Colinton people like being in a community, yet nothing rouses their passion more than the news that more housing developments might be planned. What was described in one of their reports as the 'insidious increase in new housing and infill development' is continually discussed by the committee of the Colinton Amenity Association. The outrage at the proposal to build high-rise flats at Bonaly, or have a seven hundred house development at Woodhall Mains Farm, or close the access to the hills at Laverockdale, still lingers long in the mind.

There is indignation, too. Why, with today's traffic problems, was the railway line ever closed? Why should the traffic congestion have been allowed to develop to a point when it is extremely difficult to get out of Westgarth Avenue and Redford Road on to Colinton Road between 8 a.m. and 8.40 a.m.? And then there is the modern housing – what are the planning authorities thinking of? Why are the green spaces being gobbled up by English-type brick houses which are not indigenous to our local architecture?

And there is sadness. Dutch Elm disease has altered the Dell, the heart of the parish, in the last few decades. Where there used to be high canopies of elm, beech, lime, sycamore, poplars and chestnut, there are now gaps altering the natural character of the Dell, and the wholeness of the high billowing canopy has gone. There is also sadness that the Dell is no longer a safe place for children to play or adults to walk alone. Six hundred years before Ethelred rode into the Dell, the Vandals swept across Europe and sacked everything, including the churches, in their path. Today we have the vandals of our own time, and the Dell, the church and the graveyard have not escaped them.

But there is also contentment. Colinton, although constantly changing, still has a sense of place. Just as the communities huddling into the valley of the Water of Leith, where Ethelred first placed his little church nine centuries ago, came to acquire an affinity with their surroundings, so do the people of Colinton today. Although part of the community is of necessity transitory, and although the currents of history will always buffet the life and times of its people, Colinton still has a feeling of continuity which is essential to its well-being and which will carry it forward to its tenth centenary. Colinton, after nine hundred years, is still alive and well.

Postscript
by The Revd George J Whyte
MINISTER OF COLINTON

SO there is the story of our Parish – 900 years of life and witness celebrated in this book. But let us be clear that it is only the story so far because both Colinton and its historic church live on and some day someone else will have more to tell.

Caught between what has been and what is yet to be, we can only guess at what they might have to say. There is just one certainty – that the future will surprise us as it would have surprised so many of the people who lived here in years gone by. Ethelred could not begin to imagine the wealth and sophistication of the community that has grown up round his church. More recently the school teachers opening the new primary school in 1890 could not have guessed that in a hundred years time there would be six or seven hundred schoolchildren under the age of twelve. Even those who lived in Colinton fifty years ago did not foresee the day when nine thousand people would live within the bounds. For the moment the size and shape of Colinton look fixed by the boundaries of planning consent. Will the pressure for more housing land force building across the by-pass and up the Pentlands? Can the economy and the environment sustain our lifestyle? Time alone will tell.

Colinton today may look like a village to those who drive along Bridge Road, but in reality it now functions mainly as a suburb of Edinburgh. In terms of its population it is closer to being a small town than a country village. Large scale housing developments in the last forty years have increased the number and the variety of its residents. The houses in which these newcomers (and they form the great majority of parishioners) live are of styles found on the fringes of all our cities. They range in price and size from 'starter homes' to 'executive villas'. In the heart of the village, from where most of these new homes cannot be seen, the change in the village shops is a good social barometer — where there was once a selection of family run grocers, butchers and ironmongers, there is now a video rental agency, a take-away pizza restaurant, a picture framer and a delicatessen.

It is true that the task of Colinton's church has never changed in the nine centuries now gone: it is to worship God, to preach the Gospel of Jesus Christ and to build His Kingdom in this place. Nor will that calling change in the years which lie ahead. But Colinton has changed and society has changed and, accordingly, this church will change just as it has always done down through the centuries. The challenge presented to the church today is quite daunting. There is the sheer number and diversity of the people who live in the parish. There is the cultural chasm that exists between the 'churched' and the 'unchurched'. Only now, when it stares us in the face, can we confess that the social and cultural revolutions, which have shaken every facet of society, have left our worship and our structures untouched. It can hardly surprise us that two generations have, for the most part, turned their back on the kirk.

So where does the church go from here? Listening, looking and learning might be useful first steps. Where these steps will take us I cannot say, but I suspect that they will lead us further than any of us imagine from the church as it exists today. What is absolutely clear is that finding relevant, meaningful and effective ways of being the parish church in a large, diverse and complex community will demand a high level of commitment and a varied, flexible way of working.

We who celebrate the 900th anniversary must rise to the challenge.

APPENDIX I

The Parish of Hailes or Colinton

OF the names of those who served the cure of this Parish prior to the Reformation only the following are known:

Richard de Moravia	1226
William de Camera	1378
Richard Hunter	1394
John de Carrick	1414
Nicholas Chylde	1419
James Gray	1491
Robert Lyndesay	1526
Andrew Binning	*c.*1560

The names of the ministers of the Parish since the Reformation are as follows:

Alexander Forrester (Reader)	1567	
John Durie	1569	translated to Leith 1570
Adam Lichtone	1574	in charge of Currie, Hailes and St Catherine in the Hopes
John Hall	1579	translated to Leith 1596
Peter Hewat MA	1596	translated to Edinburgh 1597
James Thomson MA	1598	died when minister of the parish 1635
William Ogston MA	1635	refused to take the Covenant – deposed for deserting his parish 1639
Thomas Garven MA	1639	translated to Edinburgh 1649
Alexander Livingston MA	1650	died when minister of the parish 1660
Robert Bennet MA	1660	deprived for refusing to take the test 1681
Thomas Murray MA	1682	translated to Kinloch 1685
Samuel Nimmo MA	1686	deposed by the Commission of the General Assembly for refusing to own

		their authority 1691
James Thomson MA	1694	translated to Elgin 1696
Thomas Paterson	1697	translated to St Cuthbert's, Edinburgh 1699
Walter Allan MA	1700	died when minister of the parish 1732
George Gibson	1733	died when minister of the parish 1746
John Hyndman	1746	translated to St Cuthbert's, Edinburgh 1752 – Moderator of the General Assembly 1761
Robert Fisher	1753	died when minister of the parish 1782
John Walker DD, MD	1783	died when minister of the parish 1803 Professor of Natural History in the University of Edinburgh – Moderator of the General Assembly 1790
John Fleming	1804	died when minister of the parish 1823
Lewis Balfour DD	1823	died when minister of the parish 1860
William Lockhart DD	1861	died when minister of the parish 1902
Norman Maclean DD	1903	translated to Park Church, Glasgow 1910 and to St Cuthbert's, Edinburgh 1915
Thomas Marjoribanks DD	1910	translated to Morham, Haddington 1934
William Mackie Laing DD	1934	retired 31st October 1963
William B Johnston DD	1964	retired 30th September 1991 – Moderator of the General Assembly 1980 – Admitted Chaplain to Her Majesty the Queen 1981
George J Whyte BSc BD	1992	

APPENDIX II
The Family of Churches

WHEN the population of Edinburgh spilled out towards the Pentland Hills and the village of Colinton became a suburb of the capital, it was no longer possible for the original parish church to serve the growing numbers of parishioners. At the end of the last century, parish boundaries began to be changed, and nowadays a family of eight Church of Scotland churches, together with those of other denominations, minister to the needs of the people who live in what was the ancient parish of Colinton or Hailes. The eight Church of Scotland churches and their ministers are as follows:

CRAIGLOCKHART:	Iron church 1880 – created a parish 1897 – church built 1899
1898 – 1902	Robert W Mackersy
1903 – 1934	Alfred W Anderson
1935 – 1951	John A R B Muir
1951 – 1961	George C Campbell
1961 – 1975	Thomas Balfour
1976 – 1985	Alastair H Symington
1985 – 1991	Andrew F Headen
1991 –	Andrew Ritchie

JUNIPER GREEN:	ST ANDREW'S – originally founded as a Free Church – iron church from 1892 – church built 1897
1893 – 1926	Norman C Macfarlane
1926 – 1938	George S Gunn
1938 – 1949	George T H Reid

1949 – 1968	John W Malcolm
1968 –	George G Cameron
1974	United with St Margaret's, Juniper Green – now known as Juniper Green Parish Church

JUNIPER GREEN: ST MARGARET'S

1906 – 1925	Charles M Short
1926 – 1930	William B C Buchanan
1931 – 1943	John Henderson
1944 – 1950	Denis M Duncan
1950 – 1955	Charles B Edie
1955 – 1961	Henry F Watt
1962 – 1973	Eric A M Davidson
1974	United with St Andrew's, Juniper Green

SLATEFORD: Created as a Free Church

1899 – 1916	James G Calderwood
1916 – 1952	James A Brown
1953 – 1962	George D Goldie (United with Longstone Church Extension to become Slateford Longstone)
1963 – 1969	William D Brown
1970 – 1986	Robert L Manson
1986 – 1993	William R Taylor

FAIRMILEHEAD: Church Extension – church built 1938

1938 – 1956	John R W Gillan
1956 – 1973	John H G Ross
1974 – 1992	Murray Chalmers
1992 –	John Munro

COLINTON MAINS:	Hut from 1939 – church built 1954
1939 – 1945	Kenneth Dunbar
1946 – 1960	George D Monro
1961 – 1975	David MacKean
1976 – 1980	J Stuart Mill
1980 – 1993	John H C Fenemore
1993 –	Ian A McQuarrie

ST JOHN'S, OXGANGS:	Church Extension 1957 – transportation of Leith St John's
1957 – 1988	John F Orr
1988 –	J Ronald Dick

HOLY TRINITY, WESTER HAILES:	Founded 1969 – worshipped in Dumbryden school until church opened 1972
1969 – 1976	Robert C White
1977 – 1983	Alexander M Morrice
1983 –	Stanley A Brook

Selected Bibliography and Sources

Andrew de Wyntoun (1350–1420): *Orygynale Cronykil of Scotland*, Scottish Text Society: Edinburgh 1914.
Balfour, G: *Life of Robert Louis Stevenson*, Methuen: London 1913.
Census Statistics.
Chalmers, G: *Caledonia*, A Constable (printer): Edinburgh 1807.
Cochrane, R: *Pentland Walks with their Literary and Historical Associations*, Cowan Bequest: Edinburgh 1908.
Cockburn, Lord H: *Circuit Journeys*, David Douglas: Edinburgh 1888.
Coulson, J: *The Saints. A Concise Biographical Dictionary*, Hawthorn Books: New York.
Croft Dickinson, W and Duncan, A A M: *Scotland from the Earliest Times to 1603*, Clarendon Press: Oxford 1977.
Cromwell, O: *Cromwell's Letters,* J M Dent: London 1845.
Cruden, S: *Scottish Medieval Churches,* John Donald: Edinburgh 1986.
Davies, A R: *Recollections of Colinton Manse*, Chambers Journal: 1911.
Dixon, N: *The Place-names of Midlothian*, School of Scottish Studies: Edinburgh University Thesis 1947.
Dobson, W S (*et al*): *Portrait of a Parish*, Macrae & Patterson: Edinburgh 1968.
Donaldson, G: *The Parish Church and the Reformation*, The Innes Review vol 10: 1959.
Donaldson, G: *Scottish Historical Documents*, Scottish Academic Press: Edinburgh 1970.
Donaldson, G: *The Shaping of a Nation*, David & Charles: London 1974.
Donnachie, I and Hewitt, G: *A Companion to Scottish History*, Batsford: London 1989.
Duncan, A A M: *Scotland. The Making of the Kingdom*, Mercat Press: Edinburgh 1975.
Ekwall, E: *Concise Dictionary of English Place-Names*, Oxford University Press: Oxford 1936.

Fasti Ecclesiae Scoticanae 1915.
Foulis of Ravelston's Account Book 1671-1707, Scottish History Society: Edinburgh 1894.
Geddie, J: *The Water of Leith from Source to Sea*, W H White: Edinburgh 1896.
Gifford, McWilliam and Walker: *The Buildings of Scotland: Edinburgh*, Penguin: Harmondsworth 1984.
Graham, H: *The Social Life of Scotland in the Eighteenth Century*, Adam & Charles Black: London 1899.
Grant, I F: *Everyday Life in Old Scotland*, George Allen & Unwin: London 1931.
Grub, G: *Ecclesiastical History of Scotland*, Edmonston and Douglas: Edinburgh 1861.
Haws, C H: *Scottish Parish Clergy at the Reformation*, Scottish Record Society: 1972.
Heritors' Minutes of Colinton Parish Church.
Ireland, B: *Chairman's Address, The Institution of Civil Engineers, Edinburgh and East of Scotland Association*, Session 1991–1992.
Kinnear, M A: *The Parish of Colinton, 1820–1880*, Edinburgh Public Library.
Kirk Session Records of Colinton Parish Church.
Lawrie, A: *Early Scottish Charters*, James MacLehose & Sons: Glasgow 1905.
Lockhart, Revd W: *The Early History of the Parish of Colinton*, Proceedings of the Society of Antiquaries of Scotland: 1883.
Lynch, M: *Scotland, A New History*, Century: London 1991.
Macdonald, G: *A Sculptured Relief of the Roman Period at Colinton*, Proceedings of the Society of Antiquaries of Scotland: 1918.
Mackie, R L: *A Short History of Scotland*, Oxford University Press: London 1930.
Maclean, N: *An Old Manse*, The St Columba Scrip.
Maclean, N: *The Years of Fulfilment*, Hodder and Stoughton: London 1953.
Maxwell, Sir H: *Scottish Gardens*, Edward Arnold: London 1911.
Munro, R W: *Rullion Green in the Pentland Hills*, Bishop & Sons, Ltd (printer): Edinburgh 1966.
Murray, T: *Biographical Annals of the Parish of Colinton*, Edmonston and Douglas: Edinburgh 1863.
Nicoll, J: *Nicoll's Diary*, Bannatyne Club: 1836.
Papal Letters to Scotland, Scottish History Society: 1976.
Pope-Hennessy, J: *Robert Louis Stevenson*, Jonathan Cape: London 1974.
Registrum de Dunfermlyne, Bannatyne Club: 1842.
Scottish Supplications to Rome, Scottish History Society 1933.

Shankie, D: *Parish of Colinton*, John Wilson: Edinburgh 1902.
Shaw, D: *The Balerno Branch and the Caley in Edinburgh*, Oakwood Press and D Shaw: Oxford 1989.
Sinclair, D: *Wester Hailes*, Wester Hailes Representative Council: Edinburgh.
Smout, T C: *A History of the Scottish People 1560–1830*, Collins: London 1969.
Statistical Account of Scotland 1791–1799, edited by Sir John Sinclair, reprinted by E P Publishing: Wakefield 1975.
Statistical Account of Edinburghshire, Colinton, by the Revd Lewis Balfour, drawn up 1838 and revised 1839, re-printed William Blackwood & Sons: Edinburgh 1965.
Steuart, A F: *The Exiled Bourbons in Scotland*, William Brown: Edinburgh 1908.
Steuart, J: *Notes for a History of Colinton Parish*, Oliver and Boyd: Edinburgh 1938.
Stevenson, M: *The Record of Sayings and Doings of R Louis Balfour Stevenson*, John Howell: San Francisco 1922.
Stevenson, R L: *Edinburgh – Picturesque Notes*, Seeley and Co Ltd: London 1909.
Stevenson, R L: *Kidnapped*, Chatto & Windus: London 1911.
Stevenson, R L: *Memories and Portraits*, Chatto & Windus: London 1911.
Symon, J A: *Scottish Farming Past and Present*, Oliver & Boyd: Edinburgh 1959.
Tweedie, J: *A Water of Leith Walk*, Juniper Green Village Association: 1974.
Tweedie, J & Jones, C: *Our District* (The Historical Background of Currie and Ratho Parishes), Currie District Council: 1975.
Woodhouselee MS, W & R Chambers: London 1907.

Index
of Names and Places

Aberdeen, Diocese of 24
Adam, William 125
Adamson, John 48
Africa 62
Ainslie, Barbara 49
Aitkine, Mrs 68
Alba 4
Aleppo 84
Alexander III, King of Scots 21, 22
Alexander (son of Malcolm Canmore) 14
Allan, Revd Walter 61, 62, 69, 71, 73, 74, 168
Almond, River 15
Alyth 45
America 107, 112, 154, 158
Ancrum 51
Anderson, Alfred W 169
Anderson, James 72
Anderson, Rowand 125
Anglo-Normans 15
Angus 11
Antarctic 136
Arrol, William 122
Athabasca, Canada 132-133
Atheling, Edgar 4
Athure, William 48
Auchingane 32
Avignon 16, 25
Ayrshire 110, 118
Baads 30, 106
Baberton House 38, 63, 119
Balerno 123, 132
Balfour, George 135
Balfour, Mrs George 135

Balfour, Graham 108
Balfour, Henrietta 108, 110
Balfour, Sir James 14
Balfour, John 133
Balfour, Revd Dr Lewis 7, 10, 101, 102, 103, 104, 107, 108, 109, 110, 111, 116, 120, 135, 156, 168
Balfour, Robert 133
Balfour, Thomas 169
Balfour, William 51
Ballantyne, James 129
Balliol, John, King of Scots 22
Bannockburn 22
Barbados 55
Barbary 62
Bass Rock 65
Bathgate 54
Beitch, Joseph 67
Benedict XIII, Pope (Peter de Luna) 25
Benedictines 13, 14, 15
Bennet, Revd Robert 48, 49, 51, 52, 54, 56, 57, 167
Berwick (Berwik) 43
Biggar 55
Binning, Sir Andrew (Andro) 9, 33, 34, 35, 167
Blak, John 34
Boag's Mill 6, 42, 82, 121, 129
Boers 131
Bonaly (Banale, Bonaley) 25, 29, 30, 32, 60, 61, 67, 70, 97, 98, 124, 129, 134,
146, 159, 163
Bonaly Burn 1, 24
Bonaly Cottages 70
Bonaly Crescent 159
Bonaly Grove 160, 162
Bonaly Primary School 160-161
Bonaly Road 68
Bonaly Steading 103
Bonaly Terrace 159
Bonaly Tower 97, 116, 124, 160
Bonaparte, Napoleon 90, 97
Border Hills 13
Borders 21
Borthwick Family 9
Bothwell Bridge 56
Bournemouth 106
Bow Bridge 45, 91
Bradbury, Lt Lewis 135
Braemar 112
Braid (Brade) 75
Braid Burn 55, 143
Brechin 11
Bridge Road 118, 123, 165
Brook, Stanley A 171
Broomyknowe 159
Broune, John 70
Brown, Isobell 74
Brown, James A 170
Brown, Katherine 31
Brown, William D 170
Bruce, Robert the 22
Bryce, David 116
Buchanan, William B C 170

Bucharest 140
Buckstone 76
Burke, Edward 99
Burn Parks 106
Burns, Robert 118
Byron, Lord 119
Calderwood, James G 170
Caldhame (see Graysmill) 52, 56, 75, 83
California 151
Calvin, John 32, 35
Cameron, George G 170
Campbell, George C 169
Campbell's Field 159
Canaan Muir 75
Canada 84, 132
Canberra 140
Candida Casa 11
Canmore, Malcolm, King of Scots 3, 4, 11, 12, 14, 16, 28
Canongate 67
Canongate Kirk 88
Cant, Catherine 82
Canterbury 17
Canterbury, Archbishop of 13
Carlson, Revd Libby 152, 153, 154
Carmichael, James 78, 84
Carmichael, Sir William 117
Carnegie, Andrew 135
Castle Gates 30
Celestine III, Pope 17
Cemetery Bothy (see Dominie's House) 157
Ceolfrith, Abbot of Jarrow 11
Chalmers, George 7
Chalmers, Murray 170
Channel, English 32
Chapman, Jan 154
Chapman, Revd Terry 154, 158
Charles II, King 45, 51
Charles X, King of France 119
Charles Edward Stewart,

Prince (Bonnie Prince Charlie) 74, 75
Charteris, John 48
Chester-le-Street 13
Chylde, Nicholas 25, 167
Clement VII of Avignon 24
Clermont 4
Cockburn, Lord Henry 69, 97, 98, 116, 117, 124
Cockit Hat Plantation 97, 106
Colban (Kolbeinn) 28,
Colinton (Colbanestoun, Colbantoun, Colbany-stone, Colingtoune, Colintona, Colintoun, Colintoune, Collington, Collingtoun, Colling-toune, Collingtown, Collintoun, Colytoun) 1, 2, 5, 6, 7, 10, 15, 16, 20, 21, 22, 25, 26, 28, 30, 32, 33, 35, 36, 37, 39, 40, 41, 42, 43, 45, 47, 49, 50, 54, 56, 58, 59, 61, 63, 64, 65, 67, 68, 70, 71, 73, 76, 77, 80, 81, 82, 85, 86, 87, 88, 89, 90, 91, 92, 93, 95, 97, 99, 100, 101, 102, 104, 105, 106, 107, 116, 118, 119, 121, 122, 123, 125, 128, 129, 130, 132, 133, 134, 136, 137, 140, 142, 143, 144, 146, 147, 148, 151, 153, 154, 155, 156, 157, 160, 162, 163, 164, 165, 166, 169
Colinton, Alberta 133
Colinton Bridge 54, 63, 136
Colinton, Brisbane Valley 133
Colinton Castle 30, 31, 40, 44, 45, 50, 58, 60, 65, 73, 77, 84, 85, 94, 95, 96, 127
Colinton (Collintoun) Church (Kirk) 50, 51, 56, 64, 65, 67, 68, 73, 77,

78, 87, 99, 134, 137, 138, 147, 159, 161, 166
Colinton Cottage 125
Colinton Cottage Homes 131
Colinton Farm 107
Colinton, High 132
Colinton House 85, 94, 95, 102, 118, 134, 142, 160
Colinton House Lodge 138
Colinton Inn 120
Colinton, Lairds of 82
Colinton, Lord 58, 64, 85
Colinton, Low 122, 132
Colinton (Collington) Mains 30, 32, 45, 73, 75, 106, 158, 171
Colinton Manse 11, 113, 140
Colinton Primary School 160, 161
Colinton Road 125, 136, 139, 147, 163
Colinton Station 123, 137
Colinton Village 122
Colinton, Waulk Mill of (see Kate's Mill) 82
Colinton, West, Paper Mill 129
Columba (Saint) 12
Comiston 6, 26, 30, 45, 73, 116
Comiston House 97
Corstorphine (Corstorphyn) 37, 44, 46, 48, 66, 146
Covenanters 50, 54, 55, 56
Covenanters' Monument 55, 125
Cowgate Port 54
Craiglockhart 21, 40, 45, 73, 84, 93, 100, 101, 102, 103, 115, 116, 133, 139, 142, 169
Craiglockhart Castle 96
Craiglockhart Hills (Craggis de Gorgin) 23
Craiglockhart House 94
Craigmillar 37
Craik Family 126

Craik, Gertrude Honora 126-127, 128
Cramond 6, 88, 106
Crichton, (third Lord of Hailes) 29
Crinan 4, 5
Cromwell, Oliver 42, 43, 44, 47, 50, 53, 61, 64, 96
Culloden 76
Cunynghame, John 36,
Cunynghame, William of Woodhall 36
Currie (Kinleith) 19, 55, 77, 86, 120
Currie Kirk 34, 46
Cuthbert, Bishop of Lindisfarne (Saint) 5, 12, 13
Daes, Alexander 81
Dalgleish, Mr 110
Dalmeny 15
Dalry Paper Mill 81
Dalziel, General Tam of the Binns 54, 55
Danes 13
Darien, Central America 60-61
David, James 70
David I, King of Scots 5, 14, 15, 16, 19, 20, 23, 27, 29
Davidson, Eric A M 170
Davies' Mill 42
de Bernham, Bishop David 16, 17-18
de Bouillon, Godfroi 4
de Camera, William 24, 167
de Carrike, John 24, 25, 167
de Meyners, Alexander (Menzies) 21, 22
de Moravia, Master Richard (Magister Ricardus) 7, 8, 9, 23, 24, 50, 167
de Saint-Clair, Henry 4
de Wyntoun, Andrew 3, 14, 22
Dell, The 5, 7, 9, 10, 11, 14, 18, 19, 24, 27, 28, 30, 70, 73, 80, 94, 100, 107, 117, 118, 119, 134, 147, 161, 163
Denhame, William 71
Dick, J Ronald 171
Dobson, William 145
Dodd, Revd Marion 151, 152, 153, 154
Dominie's House (*see* Cemetery Bothy) 143, 157
Donibristle 146
Doohill 155
Douglas, Sir Archibald 21
Dovecote Park 70
Dreghorn (Dreggarn, Trequern) 23, 24, 25, 30, 32, 45, 55, 73, 94, 102, 116, 117, 126, 127, 137
Dreghorn Barracks 126, 137, 159
Dreghorn Castle 94, 125, 159
Dreghorn Estate 106, 141
Dreghorn House 89
Dreghorn Loan 106, 124, 132, 135
Dreghorn Mill (Mill of Dregern) 23, 24, 50
Drummond, Lord Provost George 126
Drummond Scrolls, The 125-126
Duddingston Loch 88
Dumbryden 1
Dumfries 54, 124
Dunbar 22, 42, 47
Dunbar, Kenneth 171
Duncan, Denis M 170
Duncan, Robert 51
Dundee 45, 154
Dunfermline (Dunfermlyne) 3, 5, 4, 6, 7, 8, 11, 13, 14, 15, 21, 23, 26, 39, 50, 159
Dunfermline Abbey 15, 29, 33
Dunfermline, Abbot of 16
Dunfermline, Earl of 39
Dunfermline, Lord 95
Dunfermline, Lord William, Abbot of 7, 8
Dunkeld Abbey 14
Dunkeld, Diocese of 24, 25
Dunkeld, Lay Abbot of 4
Dunkeld, Lord Hugh, Bishop of 8
Durham 14
Durham Cathedral 13, 35
Durie, Revd John 34, 36, 167
East Calder 146
Edgar (son of Malcolm Canmore) 14
Edie, Charles B 170
Edinburgh (Edinburghe) 17, 26, 32, 37, 38, 40, 43, 46, 48, 54, 62, 63, 76, 78, 79, 84, 85, 92, 93, 98, 100, 103, 106, 121, 123, 124, 129, 137, 139, 141, 146, 148, 165, 169
Edinburgh Castle 3, 11, 30, 37, 48, 76
Edmonton, Canada 133
Edmund (son of Malcolm Canmore) 14
Edward I, King of England 22
Edward, Prince of England (son of Edward I) 22
Edward, Prince of England (son of King Henry VIII) 31
Edward (son of Malcolm Canmore) 14
Elgin 61
Elizabeth II, Queen 143, 156
Elliot, Revd George 155
England 12, 13, 14, 16, 28, 58, 70
Errol, Earl of 84
Ethelred, Prince (Comes of Fife) 3, 4, 5, 6, 11, 12, 13, 14, 24, 28, 35, 39, 50, 64, 163, 164, 165
Ethelred's Church (*see* Hailes, Church of)
Europe 4, 6, 15, 16, 21, 163

177

Fairgreave, Alexander 112
Fairmilehead 42, 170
Falkirk 22
Fenemore, John H C 171
Fernielaw Avenue 68
Fife (Fyfe) 5, 47
Fife, ninth Comes (Earl) of 28
Finlay, Robert 70
Firrhill 100, 136
Firrhill High School 160
Fisher, Revd Robert 77, 79, 87, 168
Flanders 22
Fleming Brothers 121
Fleming, Revd John 98, 99, 101, 109, 168
Fletcher of Saltoun 62
Flodden 29
Florence 16
Forbes, Bishop 45
Forbes, Sir William 94, 95
Forbes, Sir William (son of Sir William Forbes) 94
Fordel 106
Forrest, Sir James of Comiston 94, 97, 120
Forrester, Alexander 34, 167
Fort Augustus 6
Forth, Firth of 21, 146
Foslane 25
Foster's Wynd 65
Fotheringay 36
Foulis Estate 142
Foulis Family (Fowlis) 30, 32, 40, 60, 64, 85, 94, 125, 141
Foulis, Henry (second Baron of Colinton) 31
Foulis, James (third Baron of Colinton) 32
Foulis, James (fourth Baron of Colinton) 11, 135
Foulis, James (sixth Baron of Colinton) 43, 44, 45, 49, 70
Foulis, James (seventh Baron of Colinton) (*see* Redford, Lord) 45, 58, 70

Foulis, James (ninth Baron of Colinton) 78
Foulis, Sir James Liston of Woodhall 117, 121
Foulis, Sir John of Ravelston 29, 61, 64-71, 84
Foulis, William of Woodhall (son of Sir John Foulis of Ravelston) 68
France 36, 90, 137, 139
Freskin Family 23
Galachlaw 42
Galletly, J J 134-135
Gallolee 84, 94, 159
Garven, Revd Thomas 46, 167
Geddie, John 7, 96
George IV, King 100
Germany 144
Gibson, Revd George 74, 75, 76, 168
Gibson-Carmichael, Sir William 121
Gilchrist, George 52
Gillan, John R W 170
Gillespie, James 63, 64, 77, 81, 103
Gillespie Road 122, 125, 132
Girdwood, Helen 56-57
Girvan, Mr 87-88
Glasgow 32, 81, 122, 124, 138
Glasgow Road 97, 106
Glencairn Family 35, 40
Glencoe 60
Glencorse Reservoir 34
Gogar (Goger) 19
Gogar Burn 15
Goldie, George D 170
Gough, Captain 43
Gowan, Alexander 78
Grangemouth 146
Grassmarket 57
Gray, Vicar James 25, 26, 167
Graysmill (*see* Caldhame) 52, 56, 75, 83
Graysmill Farm 74

Graysmill, Goodwife of 52
Graysmill School 160
Great Rock, The (Grossa Petra) 8, 9
Greyfriars Church 67, 69
Grub, George 14
Gulf, The 158
Gunn, George S 169
Hailes (Hailles, Haillies, Haillis, Haills, Hale, Hales, Halis, Halys) 2, 3, 4, 5, 6, 7, 8, 9, 10, 15, 16, 17, 19, 21, 24, 25, 26, 27, 28, 34, 36, 39, 73, 80, 84, 102, 103, 119, 127, 128, 159, 169
Hailes, Church of (Ethelred's Church or St Cuthbert's) 3, 4, 5, 6, 7, 8, 10, 11-12, 14, 15, 17, 18, 19, 23, 24, 39, 48, 164
Hailes, Easter (Eister Haillis) 10
Hailes House 5, 6, 7, 9, 10, 126, 127, 143, 160
Hailes Quarry 83, 91, 102, 129
Hailes, Wester 143, 158
Haillis, Brig of (Haillisbrig) 9, 10, 33-34
Hall, Revd John 37, 39, 167
Hamilton-Dalrymple, Lady 100
Hanoverians 71
Hare, William 99
Hatton 87
Hawaii 126
Hay, John 39
Headen, Andrew F 169
Hebrides 89
Henderson, John 170
Henderson, Laurie 65
Henry VIII, King of England 13, 32
Heriot (Hiriot), Agnes of Lymphoy 11, 32
Heriot Row 106
Hertford, Earl of 32
Hewat, Revd Peter 38, 167

178

Hexham 13
Highlands 112
High Street 63, 65, 71
Hill, William 89, 121
Hole Mill 9, 23, 24, 42, 50, 56, 58, 59, 83
Holland 88
Holms, Captain 43
Holy Island 13
Holy Land 4
Holyrood 19, 25
Holyrood Abbey 16
Holyrood, Abbot of 23
Holyroodhouse, Palace of 119
Honorius III, Pope 19
Howard Place 107
Hungary 12
Hunter, Richard 24, 167
Hunter, Robert 104
Hunter's Tryst 97, 106
Hyndman, Revd John 76, 77, 168
Ingiborg (first Queen of Malcolm Canmore) 12
Inglis, George 84, 96
Inglis, Captain John 90
Inglis Green 91, 128, 138
Inner Farne 13
Iona 12
Irvine, William 60
Jack, Thomas 89
Jacobites 70
Jacob's Ladder 122
James I, King of Scots 25
James III, King of Scots 29
James V, King of Scots 30
James VI and I, King 31, 37, 39
James VII, King 59
Janesfield 122
Jinkabout (*see* Lumsdain's Mill) 42, 82
John Paul II, Pope 155
Johnson, Dr Samuel 85
Johnston Family 116
Johnston, Revd William B 149, 151, 152, 153, 154, 155, 156, 158, 161, 168

Juniper Green 1, 102, 116, 124, 169, 170
Kaiulani, Princess 126
Kalakaua, King of Hawaii 126
Kate's Mill (*see* Colinton, Waulk Mill of) 82, 120, 128, 129
Keir, George 65
Keith, George 148
Kennedy, Bishop of St Andrews 25
Kerr, John 123
Kerr, Mrs 123
Kinghorn 22
Kingsknowe 1, 139
Kinloch 59
Kirkgate 25
Kirkland Mill 83, 112
Kirklands Mansion 94
Kirkliston 15
Kirkslope 32
Knox, John 32, 35, 36, 46
Konisberg 62
Laing, Dr William Mackie 144, 149, 168
Lammermuir Hills 13
Lanark 54
Lanark Road 97
Langside 158
Lasswade 17
Lastalric (Restalrig), Thomas of 7, 8, 10, 23, 50
Lauder 77
Lauderdale Family 39
Lauderdale, Lord (Earl of Lauderdale) 87, 88, 90, 130
Laurie, John 90
Lauriston Place 143
Laverockdale 102, 106, 163
Le Grant, William 21
Leith 21, 66, 85, 90, 95, 143
Leith, Water of 1, 7, 9, 14, 15, 20, 21, 24, 26, 27, 28, 30, 32, 40, 57, 80, 101, 113, 115, 122, 129, 131, 140, 164

Leslie, General 42
Leslie, H 77
Lichtone, Revd Adam 34, 167
Limey Lands 106
Lincoln 21
Lindisfarne 13
Linlithgow, Deanery of 19, 33
Linlithgowshire 54
Lithgow, James 81
Little Fordel 32, 84, 94
Livingstone, Revd Alexander 47, 167
Loan Hall 116, 143, 144, 153, 155, 158, 161
Lockhart, Revd Dr William 7, 112, 115, 116, 117, 118, 130, 131, 134, 168
Long Steps 50, 106, 119
Longstone 83
Lorimer, Robert 125
Lothian, Archdeanery of 19
Lugton, Revd George 155
Lumsdain's Mill (*see* Jinkabout) 42, 82
Luther, Martin 32
Lyndesay, Robert 33, 167
Macbeth, King of Scots 4, 12
Macbeth, Lady (Queen Gruoch) 12
Macfarlane, Norman C 169
Macfie, R A 115, 117, 125, 126, 136, 137
MacKean, David 171
Mackenzie, Henry 58, 85, 118, 119
MacKenzie, Lord 124
McKerrow, Margaret 110, 111
Mackersy, Robert W 169
Maclean, Revd Norman 114-115, 134-135, 136, 138, 168
McQuarrie, Ian A 171
Macrae, Sir Colin 136
Maitland, Sir John 39
Malawi 154

Malcolm, John W 170
Manson, Robert L 170
Margaret (grand-daughter of Alexander III) 22
Margaret (second Queen of Malcolm Canmore) (and Saint) 3, 4, 11, 12-13, 14, 16, 18-19, 35, 159
Marjoribanks, Anne 141
Marjoribanks, George 140
Marjoribanks, Sir James 140, 141
Marjoribanks, Mrs 141
Marjoribanks, Revd Thomas 138, 139, 140, 141, 144, 168
Mary, Queen of Scots 31, 36, 37
Mary, Queen (wife of King William) 59, 60, 70
Merchiston (Merchingstoun) 37, 84, 87, 142
Merchiston Castle School 30, 95, 142, 147, 156, 159
Michael, Pope 25
Midelhope 8
Midlothian 132
Mill, J Stuart 171
Millbank 121
Miller, Jon 67
Milncroft 8
Milne, James 131, 132-133
Mitchell, Sydney 135
Moffat 88
Monck, General 43, 45
Monro, Dr Alexander *Primus* 93
Monro, Dr Alexander *Secundus* 93
Monro, Dr Alexander *Tertuis* 93
Monro, George D 171
Monro, Revd George 155
Moray 23
Moray, Canonry of 24
Morrice, Alexander M 171
Morton 75
Mortonhall 73

Muir, John A R B 169
Munro Drive 68
Munro, John 170
Murray Burn 1
Murray, Revd Thomas 57, 58, 167
Musselburgh 42
Nairn 85
Napier Tower 142
Naples 127
Nasmyth, Alexander 95
Ndomomdo, Grace 154
Nechtan, King of the Picts 11
Neilson, Jenny 149-150
Nelson, Horatio 90
Newmills Barley Mill 81
New Town 83, 129
New York 140
Nicol, Walter 85
Nicoll, John 43, 49
Niddries 37
Nimmo, Revd Samuel 59, 60, 167
Ninian (Saint) 11, 12
Niven, William 105
Normans 16, 19, 28, 29
Northern Ireland 154
Northumberland 3, 14
Ogston, Revd William 45, 46, 167
Old Farm Court 154
Old Melrose, monastery of 13
Oliphant, Margaret 96
Orkney 11, 22
Orr, John F 171
Ossian 118
Otho, Cardinal 17
Otterburn, Sir Adam of Redhall 31
Otterburn Family 96
Owen, Wilfred 139
Oxgangs 1, 25, 26, 30, 32, 158, 171
Oxgangs Road 106, 126
Paris 16, 17, 24
Paterson, Thomas 61, 168
Peking 140

Penman, Adam 120
Pennie, William 57
Pentland Avenue 125
Pentland Hills 1, 2, 6, 26, 30, 32, 61, 66, 70, 81, 84, 92, 97, 103, 112, 119, 146, 165, 169
Perth, Duke of 75
Perth, Perthshire 28, 32
Picts 11
Pilmuir 30
Pitcairn, David 72
Pitlochry 112
Pitt-Watson, Ian 151
Pont, Timothy 53
Possil 124
Pratt's Green 67
Preston 42, 44
Prestonpans 76
Queensferry (Queen's Ferry) 21, 49
Queensland, Australia 133
Raeburn, Henry 88
Ratho 77, 86
Ravelston 29, 40, 64
Redford 73, 84, 94, 97, 107, 117, 127, 154
Redford Avenue 159
Redford Barracks 51, 137, 144, 156, 158
Redford Burn (Reedford Burn) 24
Redford House 58, 59, 70, 71, 72, 89, 125-126, 160
Redford, Jine (Jine Foord) 72-73
Redford Loan 159
Redford, Lord (*see* Foulis, James, seventh Baron of Colinton) 45, 58, 70, 71
Redford Place 160, 161
Redford Road 100, 124, 125, 131, 136, 154, 163
Redford Terrace 159
Redhall (Reidhall) 1, 21, 22, 25, 26, 27, 28, 37, 40, 43, 44, 50, 57, 84, 96, 102, 116
Redhall, Baron 22, 29, 30

Redhall, Barony of 35
Redhall Bog 5
Redhall, Castle of (Rubea Aula) 21
Redhall, Glencairn of 29
Redhall, Hamilton of 43
Redhall House 77, 96, 160
Redhall (Reidhall), Laird of 36, 43, 44
Redhall Mill 82, 83
Redhall Quarry 30, 91, 102, 129
Reid, Very Revd Dr George T H 155, 169
Reid, John 85
Reid, William 80, 81
Restalrig (Lastalric, Rastalrig), Logans of 21
Richard (son of Audonenus) 19
Ritchie, Andrew 169
Rizzio, David 36
Robertson, James 78
Robesoun, Andrew 34
Robinson, John 48
Romans 1, 6
Rome 12, 15,16, 25, 76, 126, 136
Rosebery, Earl of 98
Roslin 75
Ross, John H G 170
Rosslyn 4
Roundheads 42
Row, The (see Spylaw Street) 53, 64, 86, 134
Roy, William 90
Royalists 55, 56
Rufus, King William 2
Rullion Green 50, 54, 55
Rustic Cottages 147
Sabine, Joseph 127
Sassoon, Siegfried 139
Schiller 119
Scots Kirk, Rotterdam 88
Scott, J A 7
Scott, Sir Walter 94, 119
Shackleton, Sir Ernest 136
Shakespeare, William 98
Shankie, Andrew 134

Shankie, David 7, 95, 96
Sharp, Archbishop 56
Shaws, House of 106
Sherwood Forest 21
Short, Charles M 170
Simsone, John 69, 71
Sinclair, Sir John of Ulbster 91, 93
Sixpenny Tree, The 131
Slateford (Sclatfurd) 37, 52, 101, 102, 122, 130, 170
Slateford Church 87, 90
Smith, Isobel 149-150
Snow, Cadet H 146
Sourhole 106
South Africa 131
South Queensferry Parish Church 154
Soutra, Church of 159
Spain 90
Spylaw 64, 73, 80, 81, 102, 116
Spylaw Avenue 125
Spylaw Bank 120
Spylaw Bank House 132
Spylaw Bank Road 48, 125
Spylaw House 145, 160
Spylaw Mill 63, 143
Spylaw Mill, Upper 80
Spylaw Park 63, 125
Spylaw Street (see The Row) 9, 27, 48, 64, 123
Spylaw, Upper 80, 81
Spylaw, Upper, Snuff-Mill 121
St Andrews 14, 17, 38
St Andrews, Diocese of 24, 25, 33
St Andrews, Prior of 14
St Cuthbert's Episcopal Church 130
St Giles Cathedral, Edinburgh 19, 112
St Peter's, Rome 126
St-Cuthbert's-by-the-Castle Church, Edinburgh 19, 40
Stevenson Family 112, 113
Stevenson, Fanny 112
Stevenson, Margaret

Isabella 107, 108
Stevenson, Robert Louis (Lewis) (R.L.S.) 39, 51, 101, 106, 107, 108, 109, 111, 112, 113, 114, 115, 118, 126, 135, 140
Stevenson, Thomas 112
Strachan, Mr 67
Sutherland 99
Svendsen, Talbot 153
Swanston 30, 45, 48, 55, 76, 84, 102, 106, 129
Swanston Cottage 106, 111, 112
Swanston Farm 112
Swanston, Wester 30
Symington, Alastair H 169
Tanfield Hall 120
Taylor, William R 170
Thieves' Road 97
Thomson, Adam 60
Thomson, Helen 41
Thomson, James 168
Thomson, Revd James 40, 41, 46, 61, 167
Thorburn, Dr 120
Thorburn Road 124, 131, 160, 161
Thruston 82
Tolbooth, Edinburgh 57
Tomsone, Adam 70
Torduff 128
Torphin 67, 123
Trench Knowe Park 106
Trotter, Alexander 94
Trotter, Colonel 134
Trotter, Henry 84, 102
Trotter, Richard 115
Trysting Place, The 50, 120, 145
Turkey 72
Turner, Sir James 54, 55
Turnhouse 146
Tynemouth Castle 48
Urban II, Pope 4
Vass, Bessie 52
Vatican, The 16
Venice 85
Verdun 4

Victorians 95
Victoria, Queen 131
Vikings 28
Votadini 1
Waddie, Wattie 67, 68
Wales 102
Walker, Dr John 87, 88, 89, 90, 91, 92, 93, 98, 130, 168
Walker, Revd Robert 88
Walker, Revd William 88
Wallace, William 22
Wallace, William of Bonaly 29
Waterloo 97
Watson, James 84
Watt, Henry F 170
Watters, Walter 79
Webster, Revd Dr Alexander 93
Weir, Robert 79, 89
Wemyss Castle 85
West Carnethy Avenue 68, 143
West Colinton House 160
West Indies 81
West Lothian 23,
West Mill 128
Wester Craiglockhart Hill 1
Westgarth Avenue 124, 142, 163
Whalen, Thomas 148
Whitby 12
White, Robert C 171
Whitehill 102
Whithorn 11
Whyte, Revd George J 138, 155, 158, 161, 162, 165, 168
William, King (Prince of Orange) 59, 60, 70
William the Conqueror, King 28
Wilson, David 66
Wilson, Marion 70
Wilson, Robert 69
Woodfield Park 159
Woodhall (Wodal) 25, 29, 36, 52, 61, 62, 64, 65, 66, 67, 68, 69, 70, 71, 73, 81, 102, 116, 125, 141
Woodhall Estate 70, 128
Woodhall House 66, 77, 160
Woodhall Isle 77
Woodhall, Lady of 69
Woodhall Mains Farm 71, 163
Woodhall Road 100, 120, 125, 134, 143, 159
Woodhouselee, Laird of 75, 76
Woodthorpe 154
Wright, David 75, 83
Wright, Miss Guthrie 125
York 17
York, Archbishop of 16
Zets, David 69
Zets, James 69

www.ingramcontent.com/pod-product-compliance
Lightning Source LLC
Chambersburg PA
CBHW051431290426
44109CB00016B/1516